EMBRACE

EMBRACE

Embrace the Pain of the Past, the Chaos of the Present, and the Uncertainty of the Future

OLYMPIA Y. PRINGLE

ARCHWAY
PUBLISHING

This book is a work of non-fiction. Unless otherwise noted, the author
and the publisher make no explicit guarantees as to the accuracy of
the information contained in this book and in some cases, names of
people and places have been altered to protect their privacy.

Archway Publishing books may be ordered through booksellers or by contacting:

Archway Publishing
1663 Liberty Drive
Bloomington, IN 47403
www.archwaypublishing.com
1 (888) 242-5904

Because of the dynamic nature of the Internet, any web addresses or
links contained in this book may have changed since publication and
may no longer be valid. The views expressed in this work are solely those
of the author and do not necessarily reflect the views of the publisher,
and the publisher hereby disclaims any responsibility for them.

Any people depicted in stock imagery provided by Getty Images are
models, and such images are being used for illustrative purposes only.
Certain stock imagery © Getty Images.

ISBN: 978-1-4808-6744-4 (sc)
ISBN: 978-1-4808-6745-1 (e)

Library of Congress Control Number: 2018910740

Print information available on the last page.

Archway Publishing rev. date: 9/11/2018

EMBRACE
EMBRACE THE PAIN
EMBRACE THE PAST
EMBRACE THE PRESENT
EMBRACE YOUR FUTURE AND IDENTITY

Embrace is about mental transformation, heart purification and walking in revelation. The embrace process is about our mind, heart and faith journey in the Lord.

Contents

Introduction xiii

PART 1   EMBRACE THE PAIN OF THE PAST

Chapter 1   *Embrace* 1
Chapter 2   *Fear Not; Trust God* 5
Chapter 3   *Being Perfect (My Past)* .13
Chapter 4   *Wilderness vs. Promise Land Mentality* 21
Chapter 5   *Growth is Intentional* 31
Chapter 6   *Situationship vs. Relationship.* 41

PART 2   EMBRACE THE PRESENT

Chapter 7   *Walls* 51
Chapter 8   *Surrender* 57
Chapter 9   *Stuck* 61
Chapter 10   *God's Goodness* 67
Chapter 11   *Determined to Keep Moving Forward* 75

PART 3   EMBRACE THE FUTURE AND YOUR IDENTITY

Chapter 12   *What's After Embrace?* 85
Chapter 13   *It's a Process* 93
Bibliography 99

I want to dedicate this book to my husband, my family and friends: Kenya, Erica, LaShonda, Nikki, Christine, Shannon, Kamilya. Also to LaToya who encouraged me to write in the first place and Jenaya for keeping it all straight. They have supported me along each step and I can't thank them enough.

Introduction

Does this sound like your internal dialogue? Do you constantly ask yourself questions such as: Can I? What if it doesn't go well? Am I really qualified?

Do you have statements that hinder your progress or decision to move forward or in any direction at all, such as: I don't have all the steps, I don't know anybody. I am not sure if I will succeed.

Have you ever said this about yourself: I am awkward. I am not intelligent enough. I am boring. I am not creative. No one in my family has ever done that. Stepping outside of my comfort zone—yeah right! I don't have a mentor. I don't have anyone pushing or encouraging me. No one understands.

You see everyone else's potential, but not your own. You know there is more in you, but have no idea how to manifest it. This brings about so much uncertainty, doubt, confusion and anxiety.

It's time to get out of your head. Get out of *your* box! Who told you that you are limited? Who told you that you can't? Who told you this is all there is? What are you afraid of? What if it doesn't go well? But, what *if* it does go well? What if it flops? But what if it *doesn't* flop?

Success is birthed out from failure. If you don't fall, how will you know how and when to get up. Failure is the very entity needed to succeed. The saying goes, "If at first you don't succeed get back up and try again." What if a baby never got back up again after falling while learning how to walk? We would have a lot of adult people still crawling and holding on to the edge of things because they are afraid to use their failures as their opportunity to stand. **And not just stand, but walk.**

As you read through this book, I welcome you to my journey of embracing me, my pain, my past, my present, and the uncertainty of my future. I will discuss how my biggest enemy has been my inner me, but with God, all things are possible and walking in victory is conceivable. Overcoming every obstacle is possible—even if you fall a few times in the process. Don't look at failure as a setback, but as a set up for something greater. God is up to something big in His people—in YOU—but if your thinking has been small and limited, you will never believe it for yourself. And it's time to embrace God, the True and Living God—the God that you say that you love. And it is time to embrace YOU.

> "I can do all things through Christ who strengthens me" Philippians 4:13 (NKJV)

Part 1
Embrace the Pain of the Past

Chapter 1
Embrace

Embrace to accept or support willingly and enthusiastically[1]

Embrace the pain. That sounds crazy. Usually the last thing that you hear someone say is "Embrace the pain." But as the saying goes, "No pain, no gain." When wanting to increase muscle, stamina or flexibility, there will be pain. The first instinct is to stop at the start of feeling pain. But if you stop, you will never achieve your goal. I have heard and you probably have too, "God will not put more on you than you can bear." That is how some people interpret 1 Corinthians 10:13. People say it to comfort and encourage others going through a difficult time, situation or season in life. I wish that statement were true because sometimes life seems unbearable and you do feel like giving up, but it is right at that moment that God usually shows up. After we have done all that we know to do, God can then finally come in and do all that He can do. His grace is sufficient.

> Each time He said, "My grace is all you need. My power works best in weakness." So now I am glad to boast about my weaknesses, so that the power of Christ can work through me. (2 Corinthians 12:9 NLT)

We will suffer. As soon as we realize that and embrace the pain, we can grow and achieve our purpose and destiny. "In order to gain our life, we must lose It" (Matthew 10:39).

> If we suffer, we shall also reign with him: if we deny him, he also will deny us. (2 Timothy: 2:12 NKJV)

> Therefore, since Christ suffered for us in the flesh, arm yourselves also with the same mind, for he who has suffered in the flesh has ceased from sin, that he no longer should live the rest of his time in the flesh for the lusts of men, but for the will of God. For we have spent enough of our past lifetime in doing the will of the Gentiles—when we walked in lewdness, lusts, drunkenness, revelries, drinking parties, and abominable idolatries. (1 Peter 4:1—3 NKJV)

> But what things were gain to me, these I have counted loss for Christ. Yet indeed I also count all things loss for the excellence of the knowledge of Christ Jesus my Lord, for whom I have suffered the loss of all things, and count them as rubbish, that I may gain Christ and be found in Him, not having my own righteousness, which is from the law, but that which is through faith in Christ, the righteousness which is from God by faith; that I may know Him and the power of His resurrection, and the fellowship of His sufferings, being conformed to His death (Philippians 3: 8—10 NKJV)

Nobody likes to suffer. Nobody likes pain. But if we begin to arm ourselves, as the Word says, we know that we can win. You can arm yourself in the Word by reading, studying, and meditating in it day and night. There is no need to ignore the past, or try to sweep it under the rug or feel condemned by things that may have happened to you beyond your control.

> For God did not send his Son into the world to condemn the world, but to save the world through him. (John 3:17 NKJV)

> There is therefore now no condemnation to those who are in Christ Jesus, who do not walk according to the flesh, but according to the Spirit. (Romans 8:1 NKJV)

Instead of trying to ignore shame and guilt, embrace the pain. Yes, it caused wounds, anger, frustration, unforgiveness, and maybe even some bitterness. Your "it" may be different from my "it." Your "it" could be rejection, rape, abandonment, abuse, alcoholism, drug addiction, promiscuity, bad choices, and so many other things. But please know, God is able to handle all of that. He knows all about it and only wants to heal, deliver, and set you free. Why? Because He loves you. He is an all-seeing and all-knowing God. He will use *all* the bad that has happened to us and turn it around. God never desires to see us hurting, but when we do He is always there and willing to help.

He doesn't hang it over our heads or taunt us about our past. But He comes to take the pain away, cleanse us, and make us whole. He restores and, gives us peace and joy. What the enemy meant for bad or evil, God will use it for our good and His glory. My past isn't pretty, but God used the ugly things in my life to reveal my beauty. He gives beauty for ashes. I thank God for the past because I am victorious and more than a conqueror.

We must practice embracing the pain. Embracing the pain, will never be a one-time deal because life will always bring about something that will cause pain. Sometimes the pain we feel is caused by our own choices and decisions, but even then we have to embrace it by repenting and allowing God to heal us. And we have to ask Him to give us strength and wisdom to not go back down that path.

Chapter 2
Fear Not; Trust God

"O ye of little faith" (Matthew 8:26). Who is your trust in? Do you trust God and take Him at His Word? What does God say about you and your situation? If God did it (helped, healed, delivered, saved, fulfilled His promises and so much more) for others, why wouldn't He do it for you? God can't fail. God is for you. **God is your number one Fan.** God is cheering for you. Do you truly understand *Whose* you are? Do you know *who* you are? Are you afraid of your own potential? What are you afraid of? Here is what God's Word says about fear.

> For God hath not given us the spirit of fear; but of power, and of love, and of a sound mind. (2 Timothy 1:7 KJV)

> So do not fear, for I am with you; do not be dismayed, for I am your God. I will strengthen you and help you; I will uphold you with my righteous right hand. (Isaiah 41:10 NKJV)

> When I am afraid, I put my trust in you." (Psalm 56:3 NKJV)

Do not be anxious about anything, but in every situation, by prayer and petition, with thanksgiving, present your requests to God. And the peace of God, which transcends all understanding, will guard your hearts and your minds in Christ Jesus. (Philippians 4:6—7 NKJV)

There is no fear in love. But perfect love drives out fear, because fear has to do with punishment. The one who fears is not made perfect in love. (1 John 4:18 NKJV)

When anxiety was great within me, your consolation brought joy to my soul. (Psalm 94:19 NIV)

Even though I walk through the valley of the shadow of death, I will fear no evil, for you are with me; your rod and your staff, they comfort me. (Psalm 23:4 NKJV)

Have I not commanded you? Be strong and courageous. Do not be terrified; do not be discouraged, for the Lord your God will be with you wherever you go. (Joshua 1:9 NKJV)

The Lord is with me; I will not be afraid. What can man do to me? The Lord is with me; he is my helper. (Psalm 118:6—7 NKJV)

Fear of man will prove to be a snare, but whoever trusts in the Lord is kept safe. (Proverbs 29:25 NKJV)

Jesus told him, 'Don't be afraid; just believe.'
(Mark 5:36 NIV)

And I am convinced that nothing can ever separate us from God's love. Neither death nor life,
neither angels nor demons, neither our fears for
today nor our worries about tomorrow—not even
the powers of hell can separate us from God's love.
(Romans 8:38—39 NKJV)

The words "fear not" can be found more than three hun-
dred times in the Bible. Some have even counted 365 times. That
means there is a verse about overcoming fear for every day of the
year. Wow! That is awesome. God loves us so much and knows
His children so well, that He knew that fear would be a daily factor
in our lives. Because He sees and knows all, He sent and gave us
His Word to help us overcome fear.

Trust in the Lord, and get to a place where you believe the
following:

1. There are **no limits** to what God can do *through* you.
2. There are **no limits** to what God can do *for* you.
3. There are **no limits** to what God can do *in* you.

Take those limits off. Take God at His Word. Your limits
could be feelings of doubt, inferiority, shame, fear, guilt, thinking
you are not smart enough or good enough, or thinking you don't
deserve more in life. He came so that we may have life and life
more abundantly (John 10:10). He whom the Son sets free is free
indeed (John 8:36). You have to **choose** to walk in that liberty
like the Samaritan woman. She proved it by dropping her water
pots.

A woman of Samaria came to draw water. Jesus said to her, "Give Me a drink." For His disciples had gone away into the city to buy food. Then the woman of Samaria said to Him, "How is it that You, being a Jew, ask a drink from me, a Samaritan woman?" For Jews have no dealings with Samaritans. Jesus answered and said to her, "If you knew the gift of God, and who it is who says to you, 'Give Me a drink,' you would have asked Him, and He would have given you living water." The woman said to Him, "Sir, You have nothing to draw with, and the well is deep. Where then do You get that living water?

Jesus answered and said to her, "Whoever drinks of this water will thirst again, but whoever drinks of the water that I shall give him will never thirst. But the water that I shall give him will become in him a fountain of water springing up into everlasting life." The woman said to Him, "Sir, give me this water, that I may not thirst, nor come here to draw." Jesus said to her, "Go, call your husband, and come here."[7] The woman answered and said, "I have no husband." Jesus said to her, "You have well said, 'I have no husband,' for you have had five husbands, and the one whom you now have is not your husband; in that you spoke truly."

But the hour is coming, and now is, when the true worshipers will worship the Father in spirit and truth; for the Father is seeking such to worship Him. God is Spirit, and those who worship Him must worship in spirit and truth." The woman said to Him, "I know that Messiah is coming" (who is called Christ). "When He comes, He will tell us all things." Jesus said to her, "I who speak to you am He. And at this point His disciples came, and they marveled that He talked with a woman; yet no one said, "What do You seek?" or, "Why are You talking with her?" The woman then left her water pot, went her way into the city, and said to the men (John 4: 7—11, 13—18, 23—29 NKJV)

Let's look at this encounter that Jesus had with the Samaritan woman. Here she is, a woman, excluded by the Jews (Jews looked down on Samaritans) and most likely not respected within her community because of her past. She comes face-to-face with the Messiah, not realizing that her life was about to be forever changed. She said to Jesus, "the well is deep." How many times have you said the following; my past is too deep or so dark, I will never get through, come out, overcome or walk in victory? When that mentality begins to take root, you accept and become comfortable with mediocrity. You no longer stretch yourself because it seems no matter what you try, the results seem to be the same. See the embrace process is not an easy one, but *with Christ all things are possible.*

She had five "husbands," and was searching for love in all the wrong places. She was embracing man after man, but had never embraced herself or the True and Living God. But, oh, how her life changed when she embraced the true Messiah—*Jesus.* When she allowed His embrace to embrace her, she was then able to embrace herself. She was never ever the same.

As we read through this story, she revealed her poverty-mentality and bondage by sharing about the past and how things had always been. She really didn't plan to be honest about her "husbands." She had to embrace the past and repent in order to receive her victory. Be real with yourself and with God, the Father. As we read, Jesus didn't condemn, degrade, or reject her. Jesus embraced her. So yes, if you plan to truly embrace, you must first be honest and then repent. Repent means to turn from. So turn from that sin, allow the Holy Spirit to help you to walk in victory over things that have you bound.

She had religion, she said "our fathers worshipped on this mountain." She understood church protocol, but she didn't have a relationship with God. God doesn't want us to embrace a form of godliness, while denying His power (2 Timothy 3:5). To have religion and not a relationship means that you depend on your good works instead of having faith in the death and resurrection of Jesus Christ. You may know about God, but God wants us to *know* Him. Having religion means that you follow a strict set of rules, but never truly examine your heart or depend on God for strength and power. Unfortunately, that is what a lot of people do. They err because they would rather take the comfortable road than the uncomfortable one. Even though religion can have strict rules, it's still easier than walking in a true relationship with the Father. Why? Because of Freedom. We are *Free* in Christ Jesus. "He whom the Lord sets free, is free indeed" (John 8:36).

How is religion easier or more comfortable than freedom? Everyday a prisoner is released from prison and it is at that moment he is considered a free-man. While in prison, he had to adhere to a strict set of rules: what time to get up, eat, where he was allowed to go, and what he was allowed do. He was captive, but now he must learn how to navigate life as a free-man and make choices that will keep him free. See religion is like prison, you are required to follow this rule and that rule. But to have a true relationship with the Lord you are free to choose (God gives us freewill) with the help and power of the Holy Spirit to live a life pleasing to the Father.

God doesn't force Himself on us. We obey Him because we love Him, not because He forces us. Yes, you may miss it, but you understand God's grace. With the understanding of God's grace and mercy, you know that you can be honest, repent, get back up, and God strengthens you to keep going. That is true liberty, and that is what you have when you have a relationship with the Father. God doesn't give us rules, He gives us power to walk in victory. Victory over sin, bondage, and shame! Who wouldn't want to serve a God like that?

As her encounter comes to an end (John 4:23—29), she drops her water pots. What is the significance of her dropping the water pots? It signified that she will *never be the same*. The water pots represented all that she was, and dropping them represented all that she would be coming into in Christ. She had to embrace the pain of the past, by being honest about where she was. She had to embrace her present by recognizing that she is not where she wants to be. She then had to embrace herself and future by telling others about a Man named Jesus.

To walk in the freedom Christ offered, she couldn't hold on to the past. She had to repent and let go of the old thing to embrace the new thing. She had to let go of her old way of thinking: *woe is me and this is all I will ever be*, and embrace her identity in Christ. He told her that she would never thirst again. In other words, He will fill every void and empty place in her heart, she will no longer need to seek out men or things in the world to satisfy her. When you embrace Christ, you will never thirst again and He will teach you how to progress along this journey and strengthen you along the way, each day.

I can only imagine that every time she opened her mouth to share about Jesus, she encouraged herself. The more she shared, the more He revealed of Himself. The more He revealed the more she received *His love, His healing, and His strength*. She embraced herself more and more. I bet she didn't just drop those water pots, but dropped that man too. She began to remove those things out of her life that weren't uplifting her, and started embracing the things in her life that prepared her for her ultimate purpose and destiny.

Chapter 3
Being Perfect (My Past)

almost titled this book "Look at Me, I am Perfect." I was going to name it that because my mentality was that everything must be perfect especially me, then I can control my outcomes and situations. I wanted to be perfect, but I never felt good enough, smart enough or pretty enough, etc. No one would ever know how I was feeling inside because I tried with everything in me to appear perfect. I wouldn't allow a hair to be out of place and stayed in the mirror with my insecure self. I was the *cover-girl*.

I grew up in a home with two hard-working parents that made sure I had everything I needed and a few things I wanted. Or some may say I was spoiled. My dad would undoubtedly say that I am spoiled. I am a daddy's girl. That sounds picture perfect, doesn't it? From the outside everything looked perfect, but we had issues like any other family. During my childhood, seeing my parents argue, I took on the role as mediator. I took responsibility for things that were beyond my control, age of understanding, and responsibility. I wanted my life to be perfect. I tried to do everything right, make everyone happy and be the perfect child. I was the perfect student: I met all expectations as a student, helped my teachers, and gave it my all. I didn't like to fail, and I didn't. When I made a mistake, I would be devastated, but you better believe that mistake would *never* be made again.

I had to be perfect. I had to do everything right. I had to make sure everyone was happy with me. I had to make sure my home was happy. No one told me to be perfect, but something inside of me believed that everything must be perfect. In my perfect world, no one would be upset, angry, sad or mad. No one would leave. No one would choose someone else over me. I could figure it out. I knew what to do. I figured that I could control my world if I just did everything *perfectly.*

Emotionally neglected, I became my comforter. I became perfect at concealing any hurt or pain. The only emotion I knew to display was anger. You cross me, you get slapped no discussion about it just know the end result would be my fist or hand across your face. I never allowed myself to be a child. I didn't feel safe enough to be a kid. I didn't know I was allowed the freedom to imagine or dream because all I had was my reality, which was hurt, pain, rejection and disappointment. I tried to make sure everyone was happy, and everything was perfect. My world never did become perfect. So how could I fill all that void and emptiness I felt inside? Hello, lust!

Introduced to this concept at an age way too young to understand, I learned that it kept people around and it made them happy. All I wanted was for everyone to be happy with me. I didn't want to disappoint remember, I am perfect. I was too young to understand that I was being manipulated. And as I grew older, I would have never believed that. I thought I was in control, but the entire time I was being controlled and losing control all at the same time. If lust means to strongly desire, I strongly desired to no longer feel empty so giving myself away was one of my solutions. Losing myself trying to gain something, trying to fill the emptiness. If you were happy I had completed my job, no matter how it killed me and ripped away at my identity that was already fragile, and still yet forming.

COVER-GIRL

I was a cover-girl. What do I mean by cover-girl? When you see someone on the cover of a magazine, everything is perfect, they don't appear to have any imperfections or blemishes. I knew how to look and act the part, but on the inside I felt worthless. I wanted everything to be perfect: me, my home life, everything so I perfected the Cover-girl persona. I never let on that something was bothering me, and that my world was upside down. I hated myself and never felt pretty, even though, ironically, I stayed in the mirror growing up. My sister and some family members would say I was conceited, but they just didn't realize I stayed in that mirror because I never felt good or pretty enough. But, if I could conceal or give off the vibe that I felt beautiful then I achieved my cover-girl persona of perfection. Yeah, I had the make-up on, but inside I was dying with low self-esteem and low self-efficacy—always wondering am I lovable, am I good enough?

Who am I?

Does anyone really see me?

Hello!? Do you see me?

Do you see that I am hurting?

Do you see that I am broken?

Do you see that I am longing to be accepted?

Do you see that I long to be loved?

I long to be understood, not always having to understand. I am angry. I am afraid. I am hurt. I am sad. I am lonely. Does anyone love me? I won't be any trouble. I will be perfect. I will do everything to please you—even if it hurts me, even if I lose another piece of me. Please don't leave me. Don't reject me. Don't turn your back on me. Just see me. Just love me. Just hold me. *Please* just love me. Am I a disgrace? What do you see when you look at me? I disappointed you. I'm sorry. I won't do it again, please *see* me. Please *understand* me. *Help* me to understand me. *Why me?*

Those thoughts kept me bound. The enemy had me so inward-focused, so condemned, so ashamed, so afraid. I was paralyzed, tortured by fear, insecure, full of doubt, feelings of inferiority and full of pride. Trapped in my mind, trapped by my thoughts. Self-defeating, debilitating thoughts that hindered my growth and freedom to just be me. Freedom from being comfortable in my own skin. I hated my skin, my voice, everything about me, but I thank God that He put "something" in me to strive to do my best at things. I can't say with 100% assurance that I did it for me, to please people or to get acceptance or affirmation. I can't say why He put "it" in me, but I am glad He did. When I think over what I have endured, I shouldn't be where I am in life. I was looking for affirmation in everything. So maybe that's why I tried to be perfect at everything. As long as no one saw any flaws, then they wouldn't know anything was wrong with me. The voice in my head that would keep me all bound up, not able to think clearly, and speak clearly was crippling me; and then God called me.

Called me out.

Called me to preach and speak His Word.

Called me to encourage others.

Called me to see others' potential, even when I never felt good enough or saw my own potential.

Is God calling you out?

No one ever knew how horrible I felt about myself because my life was progressing, but internally I was struggling. I was serving the Lord, but still never felt good enough; never felt qualified enough and still would have the same self-defeating thoughts. Repenting over and over again for the slightest thing that I felt wasn't perfect to God. The accuser of the brethren, also known as Satan, became my unknowing best friend, keeping me stuck. It is mind-boggling because God would use me, but I would always say if He used a donkey (Numbers 22:28) in the Bible, He can use me. In hindsight, even while typing, that is an insult to God because His view of me is nothing like what I had in mind. His view is beautiful thoughts and He isn't shaking His head or fist at every little thing I may not do "perfectly."

God is a loving Father. He isn't condemning. He isn't critical, but I was critical. Because I never thought that I could do anything to please the Father, I would be hard and very critical towards people, and that is not love. God didn't call any of us to be the Holy Ghost police. Because I wasn't happy with me, I just knew God wasn't happy with me. And for sure He wasn't with others.

I could never let anyone see the real me. They wouldn't like me—heck I didn't like me. I have been so broken, but never wanted to show that. I would never let someone see that I was weak. I definitely didn't give the impression that I needed or wanted help. I am independent. I am strong. I am perfect. Look at what I have done. I only allow you to see what I want you to see. See my perfections, not my imperfections. That is pride. Nobody is perfect, but One, and His name is Jesus.

To live a life of perfection is truly a lonely place or state of being. I say lonely because I never feel safe enough to show my true self. Also on top of that, I never allowed myself to be a child, took on adult situations way before my time, and never had the opportunity to know my *true* self. I was always the person that people wanted me to be. So it's really lonely to never feel free enough to just be. You are perfect, so you can help everyone else solve their problems. You keep your hurt and pain bottled up, but allow yourself to be the garbage disposal for everyone to dump their mess into because you always seem to have it together and can handle it.

When I truly surrendered to God people would say I was sweet. That is funny to me because growing up I was mean. Yes, I am sweet, you will always see my sweet side because I am perfect. I always went around looking like a lost puppy, waiting for someone to affirm me. Say something nice about me, say something good about me, please like me, and please love me. I am perfect. Even as I type and replay the debilitating thoughts, the enemy is attacking—he so wants me to stay in that place. Oh, But God!

If I could go back and talk to myself, I would say, "It is okay. God loves you as you are—flaws and all. He has come to make you whole, restore you and pour His love on you. It won't cost you a thing because He already paid the price in full and He welcomes you with open arms. He wants you to know how high, how wide, how deep, how long His love is for you. Matter of fact, He loved you first. He also sees down the line and loves you still and will never stop loving you. Nothing, and I mean **NOTHING**, can separate you from His love."

> That Christ may dwell in your hearts through faith; that you, being rooted and grounded in love, may be able to comprehend with all the saints what is the width and length and depth and height— to know the love of Christ which passes knowledge; that you may be filled with all the fullness of God. (Ephesians 3:17—19)

> We love Him because He first loved us. (1 John 4:19 NKJV)

> For there is one God and one Mediator between God and men, the Man Christ Jesus, who gave Himself a ransom for all, to be testified in due time (1 Timothy 2:5—6

> For I am persuaded that neither death nor life, nor angels nor principalities nor powers, nor things present nor things to come, nor height nor depth,

nor any other created thing, shall be able to separate us from the love of God which is in Christ
Jesus our Lord. (Romans 8:38—39 NKJV)

I would continue to say, look into the mirror of God's Word,
and see yourself, how He sees you. You will begin to see that all
He wants and ever wanted was *you*—to have a *real* relationship
with you. He just doesn't want you to know about Him, but He
wants you to know Him. He desires intimacy, a closeness with all
His children. He doesn't want us to think He is this distant God
that we can't touch or reach. He lives in us and is all around us.

He knew us before we were formed in our mother's womb
(Jeremiah 1:5). He knows the number of hairs on our head.
(Matthew 10:30) We are wonderfully and fearfully made. (Psalms
139:14) We are the apple of His eye (Psalm 17:8). He came down
to earth for us, for me, for you. He gave His son for us (John 3:16).
He didn't want anything between us. We can come boldly before
His throne of grace (Hebrews 4:16).

You were created for a love story between God and you.
Despite everything you have endured and will endure, He still
wants you, *all of you*. He wants all the hurt, pain, disappointment,
anger, frustration, confusion and so much more. He wants all your
heart, all your mind, and body. He is the only one that can handle
all of you—ALL, the good, bad and ugly. He turns nothing into
something. He turns coal into diamonds. Everything He makes is
good and beautiful—and it's not artificial either it's the real deal.
He doesn't duplicate or replicate, but we are all originals, one of
a kind. We can trust Him with all of us, no matter how fragile or
strong we think we are.

To sum it all up, **nothing will ever be perfect**, so *live*, be *free*
and *enjoy life*. Quit waiting on perfection because while you are
waiting on things to be perfect, God is waiting for you, so that He
can continue to perfect you.

Therefore humble yourselves under the mighty hand of God, that He may exalt you in due time, casting all your care upon Him, for He cares for you. Be sober, be vigilant; because your adversary the devil walks about like a roaring lion, seeking whom he may devour. Resist him, steadfast in the faith, knowing that the same sufferings are experienced by your brotherhood in the world. But may the God of all grace, who called us to His eternal glory by Christ Jesus, after you have suffered a while, **perfect**, establish, strengthen, and settle you. To Him be the glory and the dominion forever and ever. Amen. (1 Peter 5: 6—11 NKJV)

Chapter 4

Wilderness vs. Promise Land Mentality

The biggest battle you will ever fight and face practically every day is in the mind.

> We use God's mighty weapons, not worldly weapons, to knock down the strongholds of human reasoning and to destroy false arguments. We destroy every proud obstacle that keeps people from knowing God. We capture their rebellious thoughts and teach them to obey Christ (2 Corinthians 10:4—5 NLT)

> The weapons of our warfare are not physical [weapons of flesh and blood]. Our weapons are divinely powerful for the destruction of fortresses. We are destroying sophisticated arguments and every exalted and proud thing that sets itself up against the [true] knowledge of God, and we are taking every thought and purpose captive to the obedience of Christ (2 Corinthians 10:4—5 AMP)

Embracing is something that you must first decide to do and then be determined to continue to do. No one can embrace for you. When you decide to truly go through the process of embracing, the war is on, honey. And the war will be in your mind. Just think about it you are choosing to embrace the pain of the past, which sounds ludicrous. But until you embrace it, you will continue to settle for mediocrity to avoid it and to fill the void. The pain of the past leaves a void, and that void is there for God to fill and to heal. And let me just say, even if you don't have pain from your past, we are all born with a void that only God can fill. The enemy wants you to continue to have strongholds, so that he can keep you bound in your mind and life, but God wants to give you liberty. So yes, there is a battle, but God gives us the keys through the Word to walk in victory.

To understand the Wilderness mentality versus Promise land mentality, we have to look at Joshua, Caleb and the ten spies.

> Then they told him, and said: "We went to the land where you sent us. It truly flows with milk and honey, and this is its fruit. Nevertheless the people who dwell in the land are strong; the cities are fortified and very large; moreover we saw the descendants of Anak there. The Amalekites dwell in the land of the South; the Hittites, the Jebusites, and the Amorites dwell in the mountains; and the Canaanites dwell by the sea and along the banks of the Jordan." Then Caleb quieted the people before Moses, and said, "Let us go up at once and take possession, for we are well able to overcome it." But the men who had gone up with him said, "We are not able to go up against the people, for they are stronger than we.".... There we saw the giants (the descendants of Anak came from the giants); and we were like grasshoppers in our own sight, and so we were in their sight." (Numbers 13: 27—31, 33 NKJV)

As we go through the process of embracing there will be some giants, there will be some "ites" (the Israelites had to face the Hittites, Jebusites, etc.—ites can be sin, compromising or other heart and mind issues), and there will be some battles to fight. Will you be like Joshua and Caleb who trusted and believed God or the 10 spies, who saw the giants and doubted God and themselves?

I have doubted for so long. What causes doubt? Is it a part of our nature or is it something that becomes a mindset or stronghold? As we think about the battle of the mind, one of the major issues is doubt. Doubt is defined as a feeling of uncertainty or lack of conviction, feel uncertain about, fear, be afraid of, disbelieve.[2] The definition makes me consider again the question: Can God fail? What am I afraid of? Don't I trust God? Where there is doubt, there is a lack of trust or faith. There is also misdirected confidence in oneself, instead of God, which is a form of pride. In God, we can't fail. He can't fail and if we do fail, He uses it for His glory. In either case it is a win-win.

Doubt must be removed in order for you to have the promise land mentality like Joshua and Caleb; they were ready to cross over in victory. How do we remove doubt? Confess that it is there and repent. Like the father of the boy that threw himself in the fire, said to Jesus, "I do believe; help [me overcome] my unbelief." (Mark 9:25 AMP) Ask God to help your unbelief. You have not because you ask not.

It is so simple, all we need to do is believe that with God all things are possible. You may also have to repent of pride because, again, doubt means that your confidence is resting in something other than God. We never want to admit how prideful we are, but God has a way of showing us ourselves. After you have repented, and asked God to help your unbelief, the next thing is to feed on the Word. *Allow the Word of God to suffocate the doubt.* The Word is life, and it is key for removing doubt.

For the word of God is living and active and full of power [making it operative, energizing, and effective]. It is sharper than any two-edged sword, penetrating as far as the division of the soul and spirit [the completeness of a person], and of both joints and marrow [the deepest parts of our nature], exposing and judging the very thoughts and intentions of the heart. (Hebrews 4:12 AMP)

We must understand the wilderness, if we are going to remove the wilderness mentality. The wilderness is a place of transition, and not a place that we are to stay or get too comfortable. God didn't tell the Israelites to build Him a house or permanent dwelling place in the wilderness because He knew it was just a place of transition. It's the place between the pit and the palace. We must go through the process before we get to the promise. When times were tough for the Israelites they desired the onions and leeks. (Numbers 11:5) They would rather stay in bondage and avoid the test and trials of the wilderness. In a nutshell, they did not want to be totally dependent on God. It's in the wilderness where you either completely depend, trust, and obey God, or you will die in the wilderness. The place of transition leads to your promise.

THE PROMISES OF GOD

The Promises of God. My God…I had to pause right there because when I think of His goodness and what He has done for me it makes me want to shout! He is so faithful, just, holy and good to us. I had to take a moment just to thank Him and think on His goodness. Thinking on His goodness will also help to remove doubt and win the battle in the mind. It takes your mind off you and your circumstance and places it on Him. The more you look at your circumstances and not God, the bigger your problems appear to be.

Even though the wilderness can be so vast and the mountain can seem so big that the promise seems like an unattainable dream, you must hold on and keep pressing. Remember the promises of God in Him are "yes, and amen." (2 Corinthians 1:2) You can take Him at His Word. He is not a man that He can lie nor the son of man that He would change His mind or repent. (Numbers 23:19). You can trust Him. Again, *can God fail?* When has he failed you? He has never failed me. Things may not have gone how I wanted it to go in some instances, but it went exactly how they needed to. I am so grateful that God is the Author and Finisher of my faith (Hebrews 12:2) and is in control. His Ways are higher than mine. (Isaiah 55:8—9)

The mind is the battleground because the life that you lived before Christ can no longer be the life that you live now that you are in Christ. Please be made aware, that your mind did not get saved once you accepted Jesus Christ as your Lord and Savior. You are changed *(Therefore if anyone is in Christ Jesus, he is a new creation; old things have passed away; behold, all things have become new—2 Corinthians 5:17)* and now you have to learn how to live this new life. The war is on and it is real, but God gives us His Word to help in the battle of the mind and to equip us to win and walk in victory. We have to renew our mind. Where the mind goes the action follows. When we have a new way of thinking, then our words will change and our actions will change. We change our thinking by the Word of God.

> I beseech you therefore, brethren, by the mercies of God, that you present your bodies a living sacrifice, holy, acceptable to God, which is your reasonable service. And do not be conformed to this world, but be transformed by the renewing of

your mind, that you may prove what is that good and acceptable and perfect will of God. (Romans 12:1—2 NKJV)

This renewal must take place daily. We have to learn to not just read the Word, but meditate on it, until it gets down in us and we talk different and we will walk differently. God changes us from the inside out. He heals our heart, so therefore, the inward change will manifest itself on the outside by our words and behavior.

The Israelites show us what happens when we are not allowing our minds to be renewed and transformed into God's way of thinking. The 10 spies still had a wilderness mentality, but Joshua and Caleb had a promise land mentality. When the mind is renewed, you no longer think on your shortcomings, but the victory that you have in Christ Jesus. Your focus shifts from a self-centered mentality to a God-centered mentality. Yes, you will still face the giants and the "ites," but you know that you are going with God on your side and that you win in Him. Joshua and Caleb knew they couldn't win without God and knew that to try without God meant they would fail. With God, the battle is and was already won. God was for them and God is for us. God told them to go and that He had their back. We must trust and be confident that God has our back. They *knew* God's promise, *stood* on it, *trusted* God, *obeyed* and *moved* forward. We must do the same.

Know. Stand. Trust. Obey. Move.

Exhortation 1
Life of Faith

To live a life of faith is crazy. To the world it's foolish—to live a life fully and completely dependent on Jesus. Let the world say you're crazy!!!

> But God has chosen the foolish things of the world to put to shame the wise, and God has chosen the weak things of the world to put to shame the things which are mighty; and the base things of the world and the things which are despised God has chosen, and the things which are not, to bring to nothing the things that are, (1 Corinthians 1: 27—28 NKJV)

It doesn't make sense to your natural mind, but to live that way is pleasing to God. God will get us to the place, where we must live by faith. We won't ever be smart enough, good enough or even spiritual enough to do this thing called life without Him. To get to the next place, level, or dimension in God and in life requires faith. **A surrendered life is what it means to live a life of faith.** We have to declare: God I can't, but You can, and I will, because You can. I can in You, Lord.

Lord, your word is a lamp to feet and light unto my path. (Psalms 119:105 NKJV)

For we walk by faith, not by sight. (2 Corinthians 5:7 NKJV)

Now faith is the substance of things hoped for, the evidence of things not seen. (Hebrews 11:1 NKJV)

Trust in the Lord with all your heart, And lean not on your own understanding; In all your ways acknowledge Him, And He shall direct your paths. (Proverbs 3:5—6 NKJV)

"The heart is deceitful above all things, And desperately wicked; Who can know it? I, the Lord, search the heart, I test the mind, Even to give every man according to his ways, According to the fruit of his doings. (Jeremiah 17:9—10 NKJV)

God didn't leave us alone. He promised never to leave us nor forsake us. He has given us His Holy Spirit to help, comfort and guide us along the way. Surrender and invite the Holy Spirit to lead you and guide you every step of the way, and He will. Christ didn't leave us comfortless or tell us to do this on our own, but assured us that He is with us and for us.

You can trust Him.

You can depend on Him.

You can lean on Him.

He is always there.

He loves you unconditionally.
You can believe in Him.
You can count on Him.
He is good.

Chapter 5
Growth is Intentional

You must grow up. It won't be easy, **but God.** God is with you and for you. Anything worth having is worth fighting for. Laziness is not just physical, but it can apply to any area of life: spiritual, emotional and mental.

> Be sober, be vigilant; because your adversary the devil walks about like a roaring lion, seeking whom he may devour. Resist him, steadfast in the faith, knowing that the same sufferings are experienced by your brotherhood in the world. But may the God of all grace, who called us to His eternal glory by Christ Jesus, after you have suffered a while, **perfect**, establish, strengthen, and settle you. (1 Peter 5:8—10 NKJV)

I emphasized the word perfect in that scripture because we are to strive towards perfection. We are commanded to be perfect as our Heavenly Father is perfect (Matthew 5:48). We see the word perfect and it looks intimidating, but it means maturity. We should be intentionally maturing as Christians. Show me someone that is not intentionally, on purpose, taking the time to grow and develop in these areas and I will show you someone immature or developmentally delayed. You must focus on all three areas be-cause only focusing on one will cause a developmental issue. We are commanded to love the Lord with all of our heart, mind and soul (which includes our emotions).

SPIRITUAL LAZINESS

Spiritual growth is intentional—not something that just occurs because you call yourself a Christian. Yes, you are a new crea-ture, and to grow and mature as a new creature, some *intentional* actions must take place, such as going to church, and I am sorry, watching a live feed of a church service does not count—*forsake not the assembling of yourselves together* (Hebrews 10:25). Unless you are bedridden, get yourself to the house of God. Spend time in prayer, read the Bible, fellowship with believers, and remove things or people from your life that stunt your growth.

God told us to *break up the fallow ground.* (Hosea 10:12) That means we have something to do. We can't just sit back and think now that I have accepted Christ, I am finished. He is finished, but you have just started. You have some things to do and you must learn how to walk this walk of victory and newness that Christ died to give us. Every day you have a choice to make, and that is a choice between life and death. Choose you this day, whom ye will serve. (Joshua 24:15)

> Therefore, my beloved, as you have always obeyed, not as in my presence only, but now much more in my absence, work out your own salvation with fear and trembling; (Philippians 2:12 NKJV)

> Finally then, brethren, we urge and exhort in the Lord Jesus that you should abound more and more, just as you received from us how you ought

to walk and to please God; for you know what commandments we gave you through the Lord Jesus. For this is the will of God, your sanctification: that you should abstain from sexual immorality; that each of you should know how to possess his own vessel in sanctification and honor, not in passion of lust, like the Gentiles who do not know God; that no one should take advantage of and defraud his brother in this matter, because the Lord is the avenger of all such, as we also forewarned you and testified. For God did not call us to uncleanness, but in holiness. Therefore he who rejects this does not reject man, but God, who has also given us His Holy Spirit. (1 Thessalonians 4: 1—8 NKJV)

Therefore put to death your members which are on the earth: fornication, uncleanness, passion, evil desire, and covetousness, which is idolatry. Because of these things the wrath of God is coming upon the sons of disobedience, in which you yourselves once walked when you lived in them. But now you yourselves are to put off all these: anger, wrath, malice, blasphemy, filthy language out of your mouth. Do not lie to one another, since you have put off the old man with his deeds, and have put on the new man who is renewed in knowledge according to the image of Him who created him, (Colossians 3:5—10 NKJV)

This Christian walk and growth will cost you something. Yes, Jesus paid it all for us to walk in the victory. We have to count the cost and follow through. This is a suffering walk. When we suffer with Christ, we reign with Him. (2 Timothy 2: 12) That is the part that no one wants to deal with. People get saved and have a misconception that life is now going to be a bed of roses, but then forget that roses have thorns. We have to persevere. We must be determined. We must depend and trust in the Lord every step of the way, every single day. And sometimes when the day gets so hard, just take it a step or a minute at a time, and know that God is with you. Our humanity is frail, but God places His super on our natural, we just have to trust and believe. Keep moving forward despite what things may look like. That is part of growing and maturing. When you go through tests, trials, or tribulations, God uses every circumstance to mature us. Intentionally and on purpose, allow God to use your circumstances and suffering to mature you.

A large crowd was following Jesus. He turned around and said to them, "If you want to be my disciple, you must, by comparison, hate everyone else—your father and mother, wife and children, brothers and sisters—yes, even your own life. Otherwise, you cannot be my disciple. And if you do not carry your own cross and follow me, you cannot be my disciple. "But don't begin until you count the cost. For who would begin construction of a building without first calculating the cost to see if there is enough money to finish it? Otherwise, you might complete only the foundation before running out of money, and then everyone would laugh at you. They would say, 'There's the person who started that building and couldn't afford to finish it!' "Or what king would go to war against another king without first sitting down with his counselors to discuss whether his army of 10,000 could defeat the 20,000 soldiers marching against him? And if he can't, he will send a delegation to discuss terms of peace while the enemy is still far away. So you cannot become my disciple without giving up everything you own. (Luke 25:25—33 NLT)

It is going to cost you something. Read it again. It is going to cost more than something. **IT IS GOING TO COST YOU EVERYTHING**. He wants all of us, not part of us. He wants it all, not just the part you think you can handle or have under control, but **ALL**. Quit thinking that you can handle certain aspects of your life or control things. The very thing you think you are controlling is really controlling you. So, give it to God. Give it to the one that can handle it. What is the "it?" The good, bad, and the ugly. Give yourself to God, He can handle you. He created you, so He can handle you and everything that comes along with you. IT IS GOING TO COST YOU EVERYTHING.

EMOTIONAL LAZINESS

Emotionally lazy, is that possible? Yes. You can be emotionally lazy because it becomes safer to not deal with how you are feeling than to work through the process of healing your emotions. It is a safety net. Instead of dealing with how something is affecting you emotionally, you would rather stay checked out, or for some people, this manifests as addictions, such as alcohol, drugs, sex, people pleasing, etc. We serve the Wonderful Counselor, Jesus. He can help heal all pain spiritual, emotional, mental and physical.

Side note: Emotional and mental health issues are something that I take very serious. When you have much pain and suffering, it may take help from an outside source, don't be embarrassed about it. Counselors, therapist, psychologists serve a purpose.

I no longer believe that time heals all wounds. Why not? Because I know too many people who have gone through trauma in their life and a lot of time has passed, but they are still bound by what happened to them. Time doesn't heal wounds—God does—and the longer that a person takes not giving it to God, the longer the process of healing and deliverance from it. What man says will take weeks, months, or even years God can do in an instant. God won't force us to give something to Him. He is gentle and will continue to have His arms open until we offer "it" and ourselves to Him. Just like Abraham had to offer up Isaac, we have to offer up the hurt of the past and the emotional pain that comes along with it.

God is so good. He loves us so much. He can handle the anger, frustration, disappointment, fear, sadness, pain, _____. You fill in the blank with the word that describes how you feel. God can handle it. He won't shun you or turn His back on you. He wants us to give it to Him. That is part of the fallow ground that we must break up. Once we start to break it up, God's love starts to be poured in and we can start to embrace His love instead of the pain.

Before I allowed God to heal me, to soothe my emotional pain, I became a people pleaser. Just to think about how much I wanted people to be pleased with me, makes my stomach turn now and I still have to make sure I don't fall back into it. I wanted everyone to be happy with me or if they were around me, I felt it was my responsibility to make sure they were happy. Instead of receiving healing for my broken heart from God, I would look for people to affirm me and to tell me that I am okay. How often I would do things for the sake of pleasing man and not necessarily because it is what God wanted. It is so true that you must love yourself before you can fully love others. A lot of times I was seeking man before I sought God or if I did seek God first, if He didn't answer in the time I thought He should, I would then seek out man. That doesn't please Daddy God. We must trust that He will answer, and *be still* so that we can hear what He is saying. Also, let's be honest, He probably already has given us an answer. We are just stiff-necked and hard-headed/hearted. God's answer may not have been what you wanted, but His answer is what is best.

> "You stiff-necked people! Your hearts and ears are still uncircumcised. You are just like your ancestors: You always resist the Holy Spirit! (Acts 7:51 NIV)

Emotions are not evil, God gave them to us. God cares about your emotions, but He never wants us to be led by them. Emotions serve a purpose. God wants to heal our emotions so that we can hear clear and not be swayed to follow our feelings over what He has told us to do and what His Word commands us. Fear is a feeling and if you follow fear, instead of faith you can miss out on what God has for you. Your feelings can cause you to be disobedient, which is why you must be intentional about emotional healing. Don't allow what you feel to override what God says in His Word. Don't allow your feelings to drown out the voice of God. We walk by faith, not by feelings. Let God in and let Him heal you on purpose.

MENTAL LAZINESS

Just escape. It's easier, safer and doesn't take any effort. Or does it? We are some of the most informed, uninformed people. We have access to all sorts of knowledge, but no one wants to put in the effort to increase his/her knowledge for the better. We would rather listen to the counterfeit news, alternative facts, or resources without credible sources to get information because it's easier and takes less effort.

My people are destroyed for lack of knowledge; because you have rejected knowledge, I reject you from being a priest to me. And since you have forgotten the law of your God, I also will forget your children. (Hosea 4:6)

If then you were raised with Christ, seek those things which are above, where Christ is, sitting at the right hand of God. Set your mind on things above, not on things on the earth. For you died, and your life is hidden with Christ in God. (Colossians 3:1—3)

I heard my mom say that "an idle mind, is the devil's playground." What you feed is what grows. So if you are not feeding your mind good things, you will not produce good thoughts. *Whatever a man thinketh in his heart, so is he* (Proverbs 23:7). You have to feed your mind the truth of God's Word. It is the Word of God that cures stinking thinking, but you must be intentional about what you are thinking. Yes, you can control your thoughts. Just because a random, self-defeating thought enters your mind, it doesn't mean you have to dwell on it. Cast that thought down and focus your thoughts on what the Word says.

Finally, brethren, whatever things are true, whatever things are noble, whatever things are just, whatever things are pure, whatever things are lovely, whatever things are of good report, if there is any virtue and if there is anything praiseworthy—meditate on these things. (Philippians 4:8)

Speak out the Word and if you can't think of anything to say, say the name of Jesus. When your thoughts are not lining up, speak aloud the Word or the name of Jesus, and those thoughts will be redirected. The Truth has victory over a lie. When you get a bad report, speak what God's Word declares and stand on it. Whose report will you believe? Decree like the song *"Whose Report Shall You Believe?"* by Ron Kenoly, "we shall believe the report of the Lord!"

It seems like a lot of work to grow, but victorious living is what it is called. It is going from a place of defeat to victory. Everyone wants to win, but to win you must be intentional. The race is not giving to the swift or the strong, but to those who endure to the end. So keep on keeping on, and when you want to quit or give up, keep on. God is merciful and gracious and He understands us. He is with us every step of the way. He is cheering us on and so is a huge crowd of witnesses.

> Therefore, since we are surrounded by such a huge crowd of witnesses to the life of faith, let us strip off every weight that slows us down, especially the sin that so easily trips us up. And let us run with endurance the race God has set before us. (Hebrews 12:1 NKJV)

Choose to grow. Grow in the **grace of God**. It's never too late to start growing and maturing, no matter your age. Grow in the **love of God**, so that you *love Him, love others* and *love yourself*. Grow in your **faith**. Grow intentionally and watch what happens. Watch your cup start to overflow. Grow in the **fear of the Lord**. The fear of the Lord is reverence and adoration.

> The fear of the LORD is the beginning of wisdom, and knowledge of the Holy One is understanding. (Proverbs 9:10 NKJV)

Fear the Lord, you his holy people, for those who fear him lack nothing. (Psalm 34:9 NKJV)

For as high as the heavens are above the earth, so great is his love for those who fear him (Psalm 103:11 NKJV)

The fear of the Lord adds length to life, but the years of the wicked are cut short. (Proverbs 10:27 NKJV)

Charm is deceptive, and beauty is fleeting; but a woman who fears the Lord is to be praised. (Proverbs 31:30 NKJV)

Chapter 6
Situationship vs. Relationship

Walking in the Spirit

I say then: Walk in the Spirit, and you shall not
fulfill the lust of the flesh. For the flesh lusts
against the Spirit, and the Spirit against the flesh;
and these are contrary to one another, so that you
do not do the things that you wish. (Galatians
5:16—17 NKJV)

So I say, let the Holy Spirit guide your lives. Then
you won't be doing what your sinful nature craves.
The sinful nature wants to do evil, which is just
the opposite of what the Spirit wants. And the
Spirit gives us desires that are the opposite of
what the sinful nature desires. These two forces
are constantly fighting each other, so you are not
free to carry out your good intentions. (Galatians
5:16—17 NLT)

The Bible tells us to walk in the spirit. (Galatians 5:16) Have I
had it wrong all these years? Have I had a talk, but not really
a walk? There is freedom in being totally dependent on God.

Leaning on God and trusting Him for every step. If I am letting, truly letting God lead, then He will lead and He will direct. The Holy Spirit is our comforter and will show us things of the Father and will lead and guide us. Are we really letting the Holy Ghost do His job or are we just traditionally saying "I am filled with the Holy Ghost?" We want the feeling of the Holy Ghost, but not the leading of the Holy Ghost.

Those who suffer with Christ, reign with Christ. (2 Timothy 2:12) But do we really know what "suffering with Christ" means? When times get tough we want God to change our situation, but when things are good we don't want Him involved. Unfortunately, we have people calling themselves Christians, which requires a commitment to a relationship with God, but they only cry out to Him when their "situation" isn't going their way (hint the term situationship). That is where I was before I learned that I can truly have a **real** relationship with the Father through Christ Jesus. I had religion, but not a relationship.

A relationship is a two-way street, not just one person doing all the work, while the other does nothing. Some people can relate to that in earthly relationships where one person is committed, doing all the work in the relationship while the other person does nothing. Thank God that He is God and doesn't react or respond like us, but oh the blessings that are being missed by those who treat God that way. God has blessings in store for those who obey and trust Him.

> "Now it shall come to pass, if you diligently obey the voice of the Lord your God, to observe carefully all His commandments which I command you today, that the Lord your God will set you high above all nations of the earth. And all these blessings shall come upon you and overtake you, because you obey the voice of the Lord your God:

"Blessed shall you be in the city, and blessed shall you be in the country. "Blessed shall be the fruit of your body, the produce of your ground and the increase of your herds, the increase of your cattle and the offspring of your flocks. "Blessed shall be your basket and your kneading bowl. "Blessed shall you be when you come in, and blessed shall you be when you go out. "The Lord will cause your enemies who rise against you to be defeated before your face; they shall come out against you one way and flee before you seven ways. "The Lord will command the blessing on you in your storehouses and in all to which you set your hand, and He will bless you in the land which the Lord your God is giving you. "The Lord will establish you as a holy people to Himself, just as He has sworn to you, if you keep the commandments of the Lord your God and walk in His ways. Then all peoples of the earth shall see that you are called by the name of the Lord, and they shall be afraid of you. And the Lord will grant you plenty of goods, in the fruit of your body, in the increase of your livestock, and in the produce of your ground, in the land of which the Lord swore to your fathers to give you. The Lord will open to you His good treasure, the heavens, to give the rain to your land in its season, and to bless all the work of your hand. You shall lend to many nations, but you shall not borrow. And the Lord will make you the head and not the tail; you shall be above only, and not be beneath, if you heed the commandments of the Lord your God, which I command you today, and are careful to observe them. (Deuteronomy 28: 1—13 NKJV)

God doesn't just want to get involved in our situations, but He wants to be in a relationship with us. He proved how much He loved us and wants a relationship when He gave His only begotten Son (John 3:16). He paid it all for us. He paid it all to have a relationship with us. All He asks in return is for us to trust Him and love Him with all our heart. Wow! He will take our heart just as it is, with all its hurt, pain, hang-ups, wickedness, and pride, and yet He still loves us. He takes out that stony heart and gives us a heart of flesh. (Ezekiel 36:26) He told us to come as we are. He never turns us away or shuns us. Never throws it back in our faces, but sends comfort, healing, peace, joy, deliverance and power. My God! Who wouldn't want a relationship like that?

Walking in the Spirit is more than quoting scriptures, speaking in tongues, shaking, and running around. It is being God-conscious and aware when you are allowing the lust of the flesh to rule instead of the Spirit of God. **Walking in the Spirit is truly living and walking your faith out day-by-day**. It is applying the Word to your situation, standing on it, and trusting God. It is having your heart and mind set on pleasing God, doing things His way and being in His will. If you are in a situation-ship and not a relationship with the King of kings and Lord of lords, you cannot walk in the Spirit.

> Father,
>
> Thank you for your faithfulness. Thank you for your goodness. Thank you for your grace and mercy. Thank you for my past. Thank you for sending your son, Jesus, to die on the cross for me. Thank you Jesus for paying the price for me. You died, and rose again with all power in your hands. I believe it in my heart and I confess it with my mouth. God, I choose you. I choose to let go of the hurt and pain of the past. I choose to forgive those who wronged me. Forgive

me Lord for my pride and wrong choices. Help me Lord. God, I desire to truly know You and have a close relationship with You. I just don't want to know about You, I want to know You. Remove everything in me that is not like You, Lord. Fill every empty place, every void.

Holy Spirit, I invite You in to have Your way in me. Lead me, guide me, and show me the way. Help my understanding of the Word. Give me the strength to walk by faith and trust You, Lord, in all things. Renew me and restore me. Help me to love You, myself and others. In Jesus mighty name, Amen.

Part 2
Embrace the Present

Love Story with God

God will pursue us and lavish us with His love. The best arms to be in are God's arms. There is no greater love than the love of God. God's love affirms, consumes, fills, heals, delivers, comforts and reassures. There is nothing like the love of God. Nothing compares to it, I tried a lot of things to fill the emptiness. Everything I tried left me feeling emptier. Yes, it may have satisfied momentarily, but the emptiness still remained. Forever looking to be affirmed, and even the thing that I prayed and cried about for the longest doesn't fill me like God. What is that thing? Marriage. I was single for a long time. Marriage does bring some completion. I thank God so much for my husband. I love my husband and enjoy being married very much, and he loves him some me. But let me tell you if you don't truly have a real relationship with the Lord, you will still feel empty. I am so glad I fell in love with God first. God is my all in all, the lover of my soul, my true love, my everything, my strength, my hope, my joy, my peace. I look to Him and honor Him. How awesome it is to know that the God of the universe, the Creator, the King of kings, Lord of lords loves me, and I mean truly loves me. It's an unconditional love. It's a love that can't be measured. It's a love that can't be counted, but it *can be* counted on.

God loves you with the same love. It is an amazing love. It is a real love. God's love is sincere. His love gives, it doesn't take. His love is a healing balm. It is refreshing. It fills you like nothing of this world. It is consuming. It makes wholes. He has us hedged in all about with His love. He sings over us with His love song, written specifically for me and for you. *Oh taste and see that the Lord is good* (Psalm 34:8). You will never be the same when you experience the love of God. **Love** *loves* **you**. (For God is love 1 John 4:8) Allow the love of God to embrace you.

You were created for a love story with God.

> I belong to my beloved, and my beloved belongs to me. (Song of Solomon 6:3 ISV)

Exhortation 2
What God Says About You vs. Lies You Believe

Woman of God, who me? Yes, me. I have never "felt" like a woman of God and would kind a shrug my shoulders when people would say it to me. Why was that? The never feeling qualified enough, I don't sound or do it like this or that person. I don't "feel" powerful. I don't "look" powerful. I am tired of those defeating thoughts that are always in my mind. When God made me, He made me perfect for Him. I saw the statement "I am enough" and I thought it was silly, pointless, not worthy of much attention. As I think about the mind battles and the feelings that I have of truly not being enough, as I think about the love of God and the love He has *for me*, I realized that, yes, I am enough. God purposefully and intentionally made me how I am, Psalms 139 states that I am "wonderfully and fearfully made." If the God of More than Enough lives in me, than I am enough and not just enough, but MORE THAN ENOUGH.

Me, I am enough.

I really am enough.

I am more than enough.

Believe and receive those words for yourself. I have had a lot of outside factors in my life that would make that truth seem as if it's a lie. We can't allow our past to dictate our present or our identity. What I have gone through has shaped me, but it doesn't have the authority over my destiny or purpose. God doesn't make any mistakes. He can and will use everything that the enemy meant for evil for my good. Why? Because He is good and He loves me. He loves you, too. It is just that simple.

> For You formed my inward parts; You covered me in my mother's womb. I will praise You, for I am fearfully and wonderfully made; Marvelous are Your works, And that my soul knows very well. My frame was not hidden from You, When I was made in secret, And skillfully wrought in the lowest parts of the earth. Your eyes saw my substance, being yet unformed. And in Your book they all were written, The days fashioned for me, When as yet there were none of them. How precious also are Your thoughts to me, O God! How great is the sum of them! If I should count them, they would be more in number than the sand; When I awake, I am still with You... Search me, O God, and know my heart; Try me, and know my anxieties; And see if there is any wicked way in me, And lead me in the way everlasting. (Psalm 139: 13—18, 23—24 NKJV)

Chapter 7
Walls

Hurt, pain, and disappointment can cause us to put up walls. Walls keep the hurt out, but then they ultimately keep you in. If you don't tear them down quickly enough, you won't even realize that you have barricaded yourself inside the very walls you built. You are trapped and can't get out either. The walls feel safe, no one can hurt you, and no harm can come your way. You don't need anyone, and you can control what and who comes in and out. If not torn down sooner than later, those walls can become impenetrable. You can start to develop a life inside the walls you built, you shield your heart, and you also shield your "true" self. The person that is safe within their own walls is tough, strong, independent and controlling. Yes, I said controlling. The only thing we can control is our self, but if we are not careful, trying to control ourselves can cause us to lose control of our own "true" identity and the freedom to just be.

We were made to love, laugh, be creative, be loved and to be free. But when hurt, pain and disappointment come along we shield our self from receiving "real" love. We will settle for the fake stuff because we lose our worth in the walls. Within these walls, God's love is blocked. We never learn how to enjoy life and what it means to live in the present or to enjoy the moment. We forget how to just breathe and laugh, instead we are thinking everyone has an ulterior motive. Also, if you are like me, you wear the mask of perfection.

Creativity is stifled because the walls binds the freedom to make mistakes. It is okay to make a mistake. Go ahead and color outside the lines that is usually how masterpieces are created. Mistakes not sin, there is a difference. It's okay to laugh at yourself or use that imperfect moment as an opportunity for growth.

A butterfly doesn't start out beautiful, but as a caterpillar and then goes into an ugly cocoon before revealing its true-identity. So even though walls are not good, they are sometimes necessary for a season, but not forever. If we don't ever let the walls down, we stay in a cocoon spinning silk that will never be revealed. The world awaits for us to let our walls down so that our "true" self can be revealed. (For the earnest expectation of the creation eagerly waits for the revealing of the sons of God. Romans 8:19) If not, an important piece of the world is missing, the earth is not fully functioning at its full capacity because we are still living behind the walls. Instead of letting the walls down all at once, try one brick at a time because when we start to tear the wall down, not only have we hidden the hurt, pain and disappointment, but we will probably discover that we have some unforgiveness, anger, rage, wrath, doubt, fear, insecurity, frustration, and, of course, pride.

What will be found when you pull back the layers and tear down the walls? What do you see? What will you find? Does it correlate with what God has said about you? Have you ever thought about how God feels when we say or think things about ourselves that oppose His truth about us? Such as, I am ugly, stupid, can't do anything right, etc.

When you tear the wall down, you will feel vulnerable, but it is worth it. It will cost to be open because unfortunately, you probably will get hurt again, whether intentionally or unintentionally. What are you going to do when you get hurt? Shut down, build the wall again and become so inward focus that you never live free or breakthrough into freedom. If you do there will be a scream on the inside, there will be an internal rage because the free-you wants to break lose, but the hurt keeps you bound. We were made for freedom. We were made for love. God has given us a freewill, to choose Him freely and to serve Him freely, not grudgingly or forcefully. He wants us to choose Him. **God is love, love created us and love loves us**. Daddy God desires to lavish His love on us continually without limits, without conditions. It's a love story with the Creator, the Creator of the universe, the Creator of us, the Creator of you.

We have to refuse to allow the wall to keep us bound. We have to be *determined to live free*. We have to settle in our heart and mind that Love (for God is love) loves me. Love chases and we chase it, when all we need to do is stop and receive it. We have to refuse to allow the junk, hurt, pain etc. to hinder our progress as an individual and in life. God draws and woo us with His love and by His Word. His Words are life, sweet, filling and satisfying, even when it involves correction.

God is a safe place. We can abide under the shadow of the Almighty. He knocks so gently and waits so patiently for us to open to Him. He doesn't kick down the door or even coerce us to open. He doesn't manipulate us, but He stands and waits for us. He draws us and desires us. He is not some distant, far off God that doesn't care about us. He says cast all your cares on Him (2 Peter 5:7), that cast means "to throw" hurl that care at Him. Whatever it is, He can handle it. We can trust Him.

Sometimes that care can seem to quickly disperse and at other times it seems to delay. What I mean by that is sometimes when you pray and give something to God, it can seem like it disappears instantly with no remnant left, and other times the process seems prolonged. However He does it, we can trust, know and believe that everything we have given to God, He hears and *is* working on our behalf. It may not work out how we would like, but it is working out according to His way. I always say **His Way is the best way**, that's why we say Yahweh (cheesy yet true lol!). All glory belongs to Him. His ways are higher. Thank God for being God. Thank God for Jesus.

When we have these walls built, God can still use us, but not to our full potential. Too many people are leading and bleeding (undealt with hurt and pain). When hurt and pain is more dominate than love, your gifts are deformed and your hearing can be muffled. The greatest gift of all is love. When love isn't the source or foundation from which we flow, God may still use us, but not at our full capacity. Also, discernment will flow from a place of caution and skepticism, and wisdom will flow from pride (Are you a know it all?). Let those walls down, so that the gifts God gave you can flow freely and you can live free. It's going to be worth it. It's going to be worth it all.

LOVE VS. PAIN

I can't talk about walls without talking about love and pain. Does love hurt? Some would say yes, but I say no. What hurts is the betrayal from the person you love. When you love someone and they hurt you, it's hard to be open to loving them or anyone again. To truly love is a vulnerable thing, and it can be scary. How do you heal from that betrayal? Betrayal causes unforgiveness, disappointment, mistrust, anger, rage, resentment, confusion, bitterness. It causes you to put up a wall and shutdown mentally and emotionally. It also causes you to shut people out, even those you know love you. It messes with your self-worth when you have been betrayed. You feel violated and mishandled. It messes with your security, self-esteem and self-efficacy.

What if God shutdown every time we betrayed Him by our disobedience? To love someone is like faith, but who should we put our faith in, that person or God? Sometimes it may even seem like God betrayed you too. Cast down the lies and thoughts of the enemy because God never betrays us. How many times do you keep opening your heart to end up betrayed again? Is there a limit?

> At that point Peter got up the nerve to ask, "Master, how many times do I forgive a brother or sister who hurts me? Seven?" Jesus replied, "Seven! Hardly. Try seventy times seven. (Mathew 18: 21-22 MSG)

You can't stop at the pain and expect to progress and grow. **You CAN heal from the hurt and open up again.** God is a healer and He wants to heal us everywhere we hurt. Please be careful about trying to progress with the attitude of "I am going to show him, her or them." That is a negative motive, and for some it is their driving force. That type of motive does not please or honor God. Your motive for moving forward should derive from you truly wanting to be your best and realizing your identity in Christ Jesus. You must also know that you have a purpose and a destiny to fulfill. No one else can fill "your" purpose. There is only ONE you, and no one can do it better than you.

God has helped me see and understand the difference between love and pain. With this picture clearer, I have moved forward. I believe and decree things about my life that God says about me. I am meant to do something great. *You were made to do something great.* As I think over my life and all that I have been through, I should be dead or institutionalized. I shouldn't be where I am now in life. I am still not where I want to be, but I am on my way. The reason I haven't told my story till now is because I didn't feel worthy enough. Abuse, molestation, rape, rejection, many people have experienced it and overcame it. Humans are so resilient, if we grow through the process. I have dealt with the anger, unforgiveness, shame and other feelings that come from the things I have endured. I understand that the enemy meant to kill me, but he has only made me stronger. God turned that evil around for my good. I thank God for victory over my past, but I realized that I was still immature emotionally, mentally and spiritually.

God has used me and uses me, and I love to be used. Instead of resting in God, His power and strength, I always felt defeated and never good enough. I wasn't fully accepting of God's affirmation and validation of me. I didn't rest in the assurance that Jesus paid it all, and it was His death on the cross that fulfilled the requirement of God. I could never work hard enough to please God. We must always remember that God wants a relationship not religion. My faith is to be in the finished work of Jesus Christ. And I must truly allow the Holy Spirit to do His job in my life. God's yoke is easy and His burden light (Matthew 11:30), my confidence is to be in Him and in Him alone.

God gave me a vision of someone shoveling dirt. As I saw it, the thought came, **beautiful things grow from dirt.** A lot of things can be hidden under dirt. Don't be ashamed, of the dirt, but shine, bloom, enjoy, live and be free. Don't underestimate yourself. You lived under the dirt for so long, it became a safety blanket and to live out from under it is scary. Don't allow the unknown to stop you, but leap into it with faith and with joy. So what if you fall, trip, or make a mistake? The key is to get up and not go back. The enemy is so afraid of you. That's why he keeps attacking because He knows that you are at the edge of your breakthrough. You are free. The prison door is open, walk through it. Consider every setback an opportunity to grow. Put that brick down, don't start to build another wall.

Chapter 8
Surrender

Surrender is not a bad word. Does it mean that you lose or that you really win? Surrendering in Christ is not a bad thing, but the best thing. Believe it or not, you can surrender and still enjoy the journey. We gain some things by surrendering.

Victory by surrendering!

Peace by surrendering!

Rest by surrendering!

Joy by surrendering!

God is in control! Yes, God really wants to lead! He is the Alpha and Omega, the Author and Finisher of our Faith. Trust in His leading and His guiding. He leads so gently and humbly. He doesn't force Himself on us. He doesn't force His will on us, but waits so patiently for us to put our full confidence in Him. Trust His leading and follow willingly. He is not looking for us to be robots or mindless followers, but diligent seekers and lovers of Him. He wants to establish us, perfect us, and make us holy. He wants to take us from glory to glory. Deeper and deeper, higher and higher is where and how He wants to take us.

Yes, it is scary to fully surrender. You wonder will it be worth it? Will you seem like a wimp or punk? Will people think that you can be walked over or on? And then of course, what if I end up hurt, rejected or even betrayed? When all those thoughts and questions enter your mind, just remember Who you are surrendering to. You are surrendering to the King of kings, the Lord of lords, the creator of the Universe. Once you have that realization, you can cry out "that is My King, my Daddy, El Shaddai, Adonai, my everything," and so much more.

Trust God. It is that simple. You can't control anything anyways, so just trust God. Believe God and take Him at His Word. Believe His promises. He is good for it. He has never let you down. You may have felt that way, but God's ways are higher than ours. Only God knows the why behind our disappointments, heartbreaks, etc. Just trust Him. How? By believing, getting in His Word, and searching through the scriptures that pertain to your circumstance. Read them, choose one to memorize. Write it down, do whatever it takes to get the Word in your heart, so when doubt and fear tries to take over the Word will come forth, and bring you comfort, strength and peace.

Lay it down at His feet. As the hymnal *"Leave it There"* says, "take your burdens to the Lord and leave it there." He says to cast your cares on Me, for I care for you. Give it to Him, He can handle it and He cares. He really does care about what concerns us. Don't worry about it, pray about it. Put it in His hands. All those thoughts of doubt, anxiety, fear, anger, frustration, loneliness, discouragement, and hopelessness put them in His hands. **Surrender and abide in Him.**

SEASON OF BROKENESS

> "I am the true vine, and My Father is the vine-dresser. Every branch in Me that does not bear fruit He takes away; and every branch that bears fruit He prunes, that it may bear more fruit. You are already clean because of the word which I have spoken to you. Abide in Me, and I in you. As the branch cannot bear fruit of itself, unless it abides

in the vine, neither can you, unless you abide in Me. "I am the vine, you are the branches. He who abides in Me, and I in him, bears much fruit; for without Me you can do nothing. If anyone does not abide in Me, he is cast out as a branch and is withered; and they gather them and throw them into the fire, and they are burned. If you abide in Me, and My words abide in you, you will ask what you desire, and it shall be done for you. By this My Father is glorified, that you bear much fruit; so you will be My disciples. (John 15: 1—8 NKJV)

During your season of brokenness, my goodness, it doesn't feel good. God is so good, He will carry us through this season in our lives because there is more that He is trying to get through and to us. During that time, He is preparing us for it. He first prepares our hearts, and then He will transform our minds. When you go through this season, you come out like new. It is hard work and dedication during this season because you have to want to stay in it. God will show you things about yourself. It may be difficult to digest, but whom He loves, He chastises. You will learn to bless Him during this hard time. As you go through this season and come out, you will be a bearer of much fruit, greater works. Sometimes God may do a total overhaul or it may just be one area God is dealing with you about. You will know which one it is. This is the time where strongholds are brought down, true deliverance and breakthrough takes place. You learn more of Who God is and Who you are because of Him. At times you may feel defeated, but you are totally victorious. You will learn to praise Him through it, trust Him, rely on Him and depend on Him all the more. You will realize how good He is, and that nothing else matters, but Him.

Jesus was broken for us. It wasn't until He was broken that He was able to be resurrected and take back the keys of death, hell, and the grave. Just as He was broken, we must be broken. Once broken, God can use you. He doesn't break you and leave you. He breaks you and then uses you for His glory. After you are broken, purpose comes. The enemy wants to get you off focus during your time of brokenness so that you will give up and throw in the towel. No one likes to suffer, but those who suffer with Christ, reign with Him. While going through the season of brokenness, remember it is for a purpose and that God is with you, even when you can't feel or see Him. He is there. He never leaves you—ever. Be encouraged my sister, my brother, He is there. You will come out of this season better, stronger, and wiser. He gives "beauty for ashes, the oil of joy for mourning and a garment of praise for the spirit of heaviness. (Isaiah 61:3)

The season of brokenness doesn't occur just once, so know that it will come again. We are a work in progress. When God is wanting to get more to us and through us, we go through this season. You will learn to praise Him through it and worship Him in Spirit and in truth. Don't try to avoid it, run from it, or fight it, but surrender and trust God through it. You will love Him more and will be able to love others more.

Brokenness brings about purpose, compassion for others, diligence, strength, faith, perseverance, and patience/longsuffering. So *surrender to the process. Surrender to the brokenness.* It is for your good. God loves you. He has more that He wants to get to you and through you. As the song *"Holiness"* by Micah Stampley says:

> Brokenness is what I long for
> Brokenness is what I need (Gotta be broken)
> Brokenness, Brokenness that's what You want For me
>
> Take my heart and mold It
> Take my mind, transform It
> Take my will, conform It
> To Yours, To Yours, Oh, Lord

Chapter 9
Stuck

Have you ever said, I am tired? Sick and tired of being sick and tired. I was feeling tired of being stuck and not living the fullness of life that is promised to me in Christ Jesus. Father, what would you have me to do? God, I want my purpose. I want to walk in my destiny. Lord, lead the way. God, open my eyes. I am ready now. Lead and I will follow. I am ready to follow now. I have done it my way and it hasn't been all bad, but you have a better way—a greater way. I have some unchartered territory and uncommon ground to go into. I have to start somewhere, but where? God lead me. What boundaries? God lead me. What limits? God lead me. Who dares me to cross a line? God lead me. What line? God lead me.

One day, I asked the Lord "how can I get unstuck and move forward into my purpose and destiny?" I heard the Lord clearly say, "IT'S GOING TO BE WHAT YOU MAKE IT!" It's going to be what I make it?!? That's your response, God? You were to give this extravagant answer that would blow my mind, some deep revelation, some big master plan, not "it's going to be what I make it."

I was shocked by that response and pondered it for a while. Once I got over the fact that it was not what I wanted to hear or even expected to hear, I let it soak in and honestly it became liberating. I have allowed the "what am I to do" question to burden me, hinder me and cause me to stay stuck. Not ever wanting to make a mistake or fail, the last thing I wanted to hear was something so liberating. God has well-equipped me for my purpose and destiny. The ball is in my court because we have this thing called freewill and God will not move my hands, legs, arms, mind or anything else for me. It is up to me to make a move. He already knows my desires and they are in line with His, so now it's up to me. What if I make a mistake? Grow from it. Failure is bound to happen. Is anything a failure to God or is it an opportunity to grow and learn? God doesn't make mistakes. The true question is when am I going to move? I can be miserable as long as I want. I can ponder all I want. God has put what He has for me to do, in me. **It's up to me.** *It's up to you.*

Delayed obedience is disobedience. God is so gracious. I want to complete my assignment; I don't want to be in the way, but I want to show people the Way. I am reminded of a dream I had in college where I was leading all types of people, all races, colors, nationalities to Christ. I was the only one who knew the right way to the Way. I haven't thought about that dream in a while, until now as I type. I have a work to do and no one can do my job, but me. NOBODY, but me.

Nobody, but **YOU**, can do what God has called you to do. Quit comparing yourself to others and take your place. As the saying goes, "make it do what it do." Quit making excuses. It's going to be what you make it. God already has it laid out for you. Move forward, press into what He has for you. "It's going to be what YOU make it." That doesn't mean exclude God from the plans, but that means trust God every step of the way and remain sensitive to Him. Opposition will come because the last thing the enemy wants is for you to walk in your purpose. You may fail, but don't look at it as a failure, but ask God to show you what you may have missed. It's scary, but I am thinking it's time to fail, get back up, fail and get back up. Yes, that sounds crazy, but how else are we to grow and get unstuck. Honestly, I don't want to fail, but not moving is also failing, so I might as well make a move. Don't live life with regrets because you fear the unknown. Trust God and walk by faith.

All God said to Abraham was "go" not go 2.5 miles make a left and so forth, just go. Who knows how many "wrong" turns he may have made. When God is with you, there are no wrong turns, but some detours. In the detours, draw closer to God. It may be a win-win or lose-win situation, but it doesn't matter because either way **in Christ you win**. We win! We are more than conquerors through Christ Jesus, my God, get that in your spirit, YOU WIN!!! We never lose in Christ. We may get down, but we are never out. We may stumble and fall, but we can get back up and become *better, greater, stronger, and wiser*. Why or how is that? Because of God. God Almighty, the omnipotent One, the Great I am, the Lord of lords, the King of kings. The heart of the king is in His hands and He turns it how He sees fit. (Proverbs 21:1) We are more than conquerors through Christ Jesus. (Romans 8:37)

Thank you, God, for the detours! Thank you, God, for the wilderness because it's during those seasons that God can show us what is really going on in us. He will deliver us, heal us and strengthen us. We also must build those spiritual muscles and stamina. We must be determined to endure because the race is not given to the swift or the strong, but to those who endure to the end. It's in those times that your motives are revealed, if you are anything like me, you will begin to see that all your motives are not pure or unselfish. You will even see how your relationship with God may or may not have been pure or unselfish. Yeah, He will let you know and it's not pretty, but thank God for GRACE, GRACE, and MORE GRACE!!! He is such a merciful God, a gentle God, a good, good Father.

Exhortation 3
There is a War Going On

Warfare!!!! There is a war going on. A war against the kingdom and the people of God. A war for our lost loved ones. We need to wake up and pray that God will open our eyes, ears, and hearts to hear what the Spirit of the Lord is saying. We must get our houses in order because judgement begins in the house of the Lord. Get in position. The position is on our knees and on our faces seeking God FIRST!!! It is a position of humility and cooperation with the Holy Ghost. It is a position of love so the gifts of God can flow sincerely and freely. It is a position of power, authority, and meekness because God is in control. It is a position of faith, trust and total confidence in Him. It is only through Him and in Him that the battle is won. Our greatest weapon is the Word. Jesus, when tempted in the Wilderness, took the Word and defeated the enemy.

The Word of God is how we are established. Learn how to live holy and grow in the Lord. Like David said, "Your Word have I hidden in my heart, that I may not sin against Thee. (Psalm 119:105) We are to intercede and stand in the gap. We must decree and declare the truth of God's Word over our family, friends, and situations and into the atmosphere. The devil is the prince of the power of the air and there is so much negativity and death being spoken in the atmosphere, but it's up to us to change it. **Speak life, declare the Word and decree the Truth** over everything that is not in line with the Word of God.

Chapter 10
God's Goodness

He Knows What He's Doing

What an awesome God we serve! My heart is so full right now. God loves us and only has great things in store for His children—for those who love Him. I thank God for my husband, family, and friends. This must be what joy feels like. I laugh because I am broke, have surgery in a couple days and have some un-manifested prayers. I am not going to say unanswered prayers, because I do believe they are answered (I am just waiting for the answer to come to fruition) and it could be "no." A "no" from God is better than a "yes" from the world. God doesn't say "no" because He is wanting to hold something back from us, but because He knows what is best for us and has something better and greater than we could ever think or imagine. Even though I am waiting, I am happy, joyful and at peace. I feel it bubbling up inside of me, and I don't want it to leave.

The joy of the Lord is my strength. I could be wrong, but I have come to realize that statement is reality only when God is your source, center and everything. When you make God your source, you will have the strength to get through whatever comes your way. When you are totally dependent on Him, and you know that you know He is for you and only has good things in store, it brings peace and joy, and then strength arises. The strength to continue to trust Him and decree His promises despite how you feel or despite your situation. Strength to keep going.

To have true joy, you must have faith in God and stand on His Word and His character. Fight for your joy and peace every day because the enemy will try to steal it. Joy gives you the strength to keep pressing forward despite your circumstance. Peace helps you to keep trusting God because you know He can't and won't fail. Rejoice and again I say rejoice. (Philippians 4:4) Keep declaring His goodness and faithfulness because when you do, it keeps you encouraged. Praise confuses the enemy. Our circumstances doesn't change who God is. It doesn't change His character. If anything, it changes us; it makes us more like Him. God takes care of His own, He said He would and He does. He is faithful, even to the faithless. He won't go against His name and it remains forever. His name is not just a name, but it's Who He is. He is "I Am that I Am." Do we truly understand Who we serve, who our Daddy is? He is a good, good Father. He never leaves us, nor forsakes us. We may not feel Him, but faith doesn't require feelings, it requires trust, confidence, and total dependence on God.

SEEK FIRST THE KINGDOM

What will save us from headaches and heartbreak is to follow the simple instruction that Jesus gave us in Matthew 6:33, "but, seek ye first the Kingdom of God and His righteousness." It doesn't just say Seek ye first, it says BUT Seek ye first. We can't skip the "but" because right before the passage Jesus is saying God knows the things that you have need of. *Don't worry.* Instead of focusing and worrying about your needs, **seek Him first.**

Seek Him and trust Him. He has our best interest at heart and in mind. He knows the plans He has for us (Jeremiah 29:11). Believe and receive it. We need a Proverbs 3:5-6 mentality: *Trust in the LORD with all your heart, and lean not on your own un-derstanding, in all your ways acknowledge Him, and He shall direct your paths.* If this is not our mindset, we get in God's way, move ahead of Him and block the blessings that He is trying to get to us. How many times have we needed money for a bill, and instead of waiting on God we went to a quick loan or borrowed the money from someone or somewhere else? I am guilty which is why I can attest to it. I don't know what God may have had planned, but because I didn't wait, I missed the blessing. What are we to do during those times when it's the midnight hour and it doesn't seem as if God is going to come through? Pray and ask for wisdom. Also repent because we didn't follow the main thing, which is seeking Him first. If we would have sought Him first, we probably wouldn't have that debt or issue in the first place.

I know it works, if we just trust Him and try Him. I had a situa-tion where my account was in the negative and I didn't have enough cash to cover it or my bills. I kept decreeing God's Word, and cast-ing down thoughts and imaginations while driving to the bank. I go into the bank and talked with the manager. He removed the deficit and money was added into my account. Again, my account was in the negative and the bank put money in my account above and beyond. God is good!!!! Exceedingly and abundantly (Ephesians 3:20) is how He blesses His children. Thank God for His faithful-ness. He probably just shakes his head at our humanness and flesh because He knows that He has something far greater, but we settle for the "right now" instead waiting patiently on the Lord.

Can God depend on us to do with the blessing what He would have us to do? We may be the vessel that God wants to use to be the blessing. It could be our selfishness that is blocking us from being blessed to bless someone else. Even though we are blessed and still receive blessings from God, there is so much more. That is a kingdom mind. We are King's kids. We have an inheritance, we are joint-heirs, and we are sons and daughters. We call Him

King and Lord, but also Abba "papa." We must get this, God is wanting to change our perception, point of view, and position in terms of the Kingdom. In God, there is no lack. He gives us power to get wealth. (Deuteronomy 8:18) Seek Him first, and He will give us the wisdom and kingdom ideas, provide the provision and favor. God is awesome and all knowing. He wants our active participation because faith without works is dead. (James 2:17)

God wants to walk with us in a close intimate way. Not just when we need something, but daily. Think about it, He walked and talked with Adam in the cool of the day in the garden. (Genesis 3:8)That's the relationship He desires to have with us, that is why He gave His only begotten Son. That is why the Word says to pray without ceasing in other words don't stop communicating with God at any point. Also, don't do all the talking, but listen.

The veil was torn so that we can come boldly before the throne of grace (Hebrew 4:16). That is so awesome, thank you Jesus. We can come as we are to Daddy God. He is for us, and He loves us with a love that is so unconditional that we will never ever be able to comprehend it all. He put it all on the cross. There is no one else we can trust or fully abandon ourselves to. God's only motive is to love us. All God wants to do is love us. All we want is love, right? Allow the love of God to permeate and penetrate your heart and satisfy you like nothing of this world. God's love is the only love that doesn't hurt or disappoint. Yes, it may feel like it is hurting us when it's not going our way, but when we are ready to see it, we will see that "His" way will always be the best way. Even when He is correcting us and saying no, it's for the best. God's "no" is better than the world's yes any day.

CHILD OF THE KING

Knowing that you are a son/daughter of God comes with boldness and confidence. God doesn't forsake His own. He is for us. I have power and authority. I don't have to settle for less than or live a life other than blessed. That doesn't mean I am high-minded or have everything I want, but I have everything I need. He will give me wisdom and knowledge. I am royalty, a chosen generation (1 Peter 2:9). I am a citizen of heaven, Christ Ambassador (2 Corinthians 5:20). I am who God says I am. I can have what God says I can have. I can do what He says I can do. As a daughter of the King with a kingdom mind, my language must reflect it, my behavior and my life must reflect it. I am Daddy's girl! Do I see Him, when I look at me? I should because He sees Himself when He looks at me because the blood has been applied. The blood has cleansed me and made me whole. So, as a daughter, I can release the pain from the past, trust God with my present and embrace who I am and Whose I am and walk into my purpose and destiny.

Purpose and destiny can only truly be fulfilled when you embrace your identity in Christ, relinquish control, and trust Him totally. Why is that? Because then your only motive will be to please your Father, Daddy God. It's for Him. It's all about Him. Thank you Lord for the pain, storms past, storms present, and storms to come because ultimately it will bring You the glory. It will reveal Your goodness, it will continue to transform and renew my mind and make me more and more like You.

That's what I plan to embrace from this point on. Embracing Abba, papa. Embracing my God. Embracing my inheritance. Embracing my identity. *Embracing my pain, but only through my praise.* What the enemy has meant for bad, God has turned it for my good according to His purpose.

Exhortation 4
Lead with Faith

L et faith be your first response. For myself, I am working on keeping things simple. We are to seek Him first and we should have our faith at the forefront. My norm was to stress, worry and analyze it to figure it out. I would also pray about it, but my faith would always be lacking. The Word says "NOW" Faith is. (Hebrew 11:1) That means in every instance, in every situation, and circumstance faith is that substance of things hoped for the evidence of things not seen (Hebrew 11:1). It's not what you go to, just in case this or that? But, **faith is now, now is faith.** Life will be so much simpler if we would grab ahold of our faith in Christ Jesus and keep it front and center. There is power in the cross. The cross was never an afterthought to God, so our faith should never be an afterthought to us. Go through it (your struggle, test, trial, tribulation, etc.) in faith. Keep walking in faith. Live by faith. Now faith is. Build yourselves up on your most holy faith. Without faith, it is impossible to please the Father (Hebrew 11:6). Now faith is. Not later faith is. _Now_ faith is.

Chapter 11
Determined to Keep Moving Forward

The enemy wants me to go back, but I refuse. My flesh will die and I will trust God. The battle is the Lord's and I will not give my energy to the enemy, he can't have my joy, peace, or my mind. He is a liar and a deceiver. God really does have my back and I choose to let him fight my battle. I choose to allow Him to take care of my enemies. People should be careful about who they talk negatively about and the confusion they try to stir up when it comes to the saints of God because God doesn't play about His children. The hard thing for us to do as children of God, is to truly trust Him enough to handle it and not allow our flesh to take control. Listen for God's voice and leading about what to do because He can and will instruct us on what to do. Remember, **God is our avenger.**

I am a child of God. Have we ever just thought about that statement and its meaning or the power of it? It's not just a title, it's not just a religious saying. When you accept Christ as your Lord and Savior, you are now a new creature, joint heirs with Him, and a child of God.

> And since we are his children, we are his heirs. In fact, together with Christ we are heirs of God's glory. But if we are to share his glory, we must also share his suffering. (Romans 8:17 NKJV)

For you are all sons of God through faith in Christ Jesus. For as many of you as were baptized into Christ have put on Christ. There is neither Jew nor Greek, there is neither slave nor free, there is neither male nor female; for you are all one in Christ Jesus. And if you are Christ's, then you are Abraham's seed, and heirs according to the promise. (Galatians 3:26—29 NKJV)

And because you are sons, God has sent forth the Spirit of His Son into your hearts, crying out, "Abba, Father!" Therefore you are no longer a slave but a son, and if a son, then an heir of God through Christ. (Galatians 4:6—7 NKJV)

As a child of God, you have an inheritance, authority and access into the Kingdom of God. You have protection and access to everything you need to fulfill your purpose and destiny. You also have authority over the enemy and the last thing he wants is for a child of God to truly understand their identity, Whose they are and who they are in Christ. Once a person gets ahold of that truth, the enemy can't keep them bound. Yes, he will continue to attack. The weapon will form, but it won't prosper. When the attack comes, the first response will not be to step back, but to stand and step up. Just like Jesus in the wilderness, He refuted every argument with the Word of His Father and the enemy went away. Adam and Eve in the garden believed the lie, but Jesus spoke the truth and overpowered the enemy. What did God say? What did my Daddy say?

We have to get a true understanding of our identity in Christ. We have a confused generation out there in this world and they need people who know Whose they are and who they are to help them. When we know our true identity then we understand:

- The power of our words.
- The cost of obedience as well as disobedience.
- The reason why we must die to our flesh daily.
- The reason why we must seek the kingdom first.
- And why faith and love and truth are vital to victorious living.

We won't allow every little bit of adversity to shake us or move us, but we will be immovable (1 Corinthians 15:58). Our gifts and our talents will glorify God and will lift up the kingdom and favor will come. Our vision will be clearer and we will be single-minded in our pursuits because we will **pursue Him**. We will no longer seek to please people, but God and God alone. We will hunger and thirst for righteousness, we will not want anything in our life that will cause separation from Daddy God. Sin separates us from God—the wages of sin is death (Romans 6:23). We will be desperate to expand the kingdom and see others come to the knowledge of Jesus Christ. We will get rid of selfish ambition and ulterior motives because our desire will be to please the Father. Our desires will be His desires. We will welcome the times of pruning and rejoice in tribulations.

THE ENEMY NEVER STOPS TRYING TO DISTRACT AND DISCOURAGE US

The war continues. The warfare is real because the enemy comes to steal, kill and destroy. (John 10:10) He loves to try to discourage us and distract us from God and from our purpose in the earth. Discouragement is real, but like David, we have to learn to encourage ourselves. (1 Samuel 30:6) Stop looking to the right or left because when we do everything seems overwhelming and impossible. God says, "through Him all things are possible." Walk by faith and not by sight. Be alert and watchful when discouragement is creeping in. Begin to create an atmosphere by praising and worshipping God, and reading the Word. It is the Truth that makes us free; and God inhabits the praises of His people—not our complaints, but our praise. Continue to have a praise on your lips because praise is a weapon against the enemy and it makes room for God to work on our behalf. We must tell our problems how big our God is, and not complain to God about how big our problems appear to be. The Word says to build yourself up on your most holy faith (Jude 20).

I am determined to finish my course. The race is not given to the quick or strong, but to those who endure to the end (1 Corinthians 9:24—27). Thank you Lord for the testing and stretching.

> My brethren, count it all joy when you fall into various trials, knowing that the testing of your faith produces patience. But let patience have its perfect work, that you may be perfect and complete, lacking nothing. (James 1:2—4 NKJV)

I am not giving up or giving in, I will finish the course. I will be steadfast. I will do everything God has called me to do. I want my destiny. To get to your destiny is a fight because the world is against you, but God is for you and all things are possible through Him. **All hell is against you, but all heaven is for you!** You are on the winning team with Daddy God! The warfare is building our spiritual muscles. It's easier to take flight than to fight. I am a champion. I am victorious because I can do all things through Christ Jesus which strengthens me (Philippians 4:13). It's true, that whatever doesn't break you, makes you stronger. I am going all the way. Yet in all these things I am more than a conqueror (Romans 8:37). We overcome discouragement through the power of the Word, speaking and declaring the truth of God's Word.

We have authority. We have power. God puts His super on our natural. We are spiritual beings.

When you make your mind up and decree what you are going to do, the enemy continues to try to stop your progress and forward movement. What God has for us is so much bigger than us. The last thing the devil wants is for us to walk in our purpose into our destiny. We can't be fearful and we can't be anxious for NOTHING!!! God has our back, and is for us. He only thinks good thoughts towards us. I was listening to a song and the singer was singing "don't talk about a child of the king, because my Daddy sits up on the throne," and then he went on to say, "I am bold as a lion because my Daddy sits up on the throne." (Gospel Artist Todd Dulaney "The Anthem") That song began to encourage me and reminded me of Whose I am and who I am because of Whose I am. Declare, "I AM BOLD AS A LION BECAUSE MY DADDY SITS UP ON THE THRONE."

> Yet in all these things we are more than conquerors through Him who loved us. (Romans 8:37 NKJV)

> For I know the thoughts that I think toward you, says the Lord, thoughts of peace and not of evil, to give you a future and a hope. (Jeremiah 29:11 NKJV)

> For God has not given us a spirit of fear, but of power and of love and of a sound mind. (2 Timothy 1:7 NKJV)

> Be anxious for nothing, but in everything by prayer and supplication, with thanksgiving, let your requests be made known to God; and the

peace of God, which surpasses all understanding,
will guard your hearts and minds through Christ
Jesus (Philippians 4:6— NKJV 7)

We have to proclaim what God says about us and cast down
every thought and imaginations that exalts itself against the
knowledge of God. (2 Corinthians 10:3-5). The enemy is so afraid
of the children of God, but he has deceived us to the point that we
are more afraid of him. We have power and authority over him.
Jesus said we "have power over the enemy, to trample upon ser-
pents and scorpions," but that does come with some stipulations.
The requirement is that our names are written in heaven. If our
names are not written in heaven, we will be like the sons of Sceva.

Behold, I give you the authority to trample on ser-
pents and scorpions, and over all the power of the
enemy, and nothing shall by any means hurt you.
Nevertheless do not rejoice in this, that the spirits
are subject to you, but rather rejoice because your
names are written in heaven." (Luke 10:19—20
NKJV)

Seven sons of a Jewish high priest named Sceva
were doing this. But the evil spirit answered them,
"Jesus I know, and Paul I recognize, but who are
you?" And the man in whom was the evil spirit
leaped on them, mastered all of them and overpowered them, so that they fled out of that house
naked and wounded. (Acts 19: 14—16 NKJV)

To get what God has for us, we need to stand on His Word,
walk in His Promises and move forward. We have to quit allowing
ourselves to get distracted and consumed with the world. Take

God at His Word and trust Him. He can't fail. He won't fail. We may and will fail, but in God a failure is a blessing. It allows God to build something in us, makes us stronger and more confident in Him. That failure will cause us to look at ourselves and do a check-up to make sure that we are trusting, walking in faith, and seeking Him first.(Examine yourselves *as to* whether you are in the faith. Test yourselves. 2 Corinthians 13:5)

We must press past the pain and embrace our purpose. Embrace the pain first. Why embrace it? Because you have to recognize that it's there and not ignore it. So yes, acknowledge that you hurt, that this is hard, that someone hurt you, that is how you embrace it, but then recognize what God says about you and your situation. Each time he said, "My grace is all you need. My power works best in weakness."(2 Corinthians 12:9) Like Paul, I can now say that I am glad to boast about my weaknesses, so that the power of Christ can work through me (2 Corinthians 12:9). After you embrace that truth, you can release the pain and then embrace the promises of God. His promises are yes and amen! If He said it, He can and will do it! We can be confident about that. He is on our side. He is our Daddy. He has our back and has us covered all around about.

Daddy,

Thank you! Thank you for all you do, all you have done and all you will do. Thank You, thank You. You are so good and faithful. You have been better to me, than I have been to myself. God I desire to be more like you. I am determined to follow you with my whole heart. Forgive me Lord for letting the past and my current circumstances get in the way of my relationship with You. Forgive me of my sins. Reveal those hidden sins. Give me strength, oh God, to walk by faith and not by sight. Satan, I rebuke you, and cancel every assignment. I plead the blood of Jesus. No weapon formed against me shall prosper and every tongue that may rise I will condemn. God, You are my strength. You are my hope. I depend on You Lord for all things. Help me to love. Holy Spirit, fill me again. Thank you, that I can do all things through Christ that strengthens me. I press forward, and will not look back any longer. I thank you for the testing. Rain on me Lord and consume me. I ask for wisdom Lord. I want my destiny and I am determined to walk in my purpose. God, it's all about You and not about me. Be glorified and be magnified. In Jesus' Mighty name. Amen.

Part 3
Embrace the Future and Your Identity

Chapter 12
What's After Embrace?

How do you embrace? Repent, let go, trust, pray, worship, praise, and get in the Word. Decree and declare freedom and His Word over your life. Embrace God. Know and understand the love of God. Stop trying to fix yourself and trust the finished work of the cross. He said, "It is finished." (John 19:30) The only thing left for you to do is obey God and take Him at His Word. Yeah, your situation may be rough and seems dim, but Jesus is the Way, Truth and the Life, and the Light of the World. Embrace this race, be a good soldier. We are kings and priests, yes, we will go to war, but the battle is already won. Tis so sweet to trust in Jesus.

I want to have everything God has for me. I rebuke the mindset of a slave and wilderness thinking and say what God says about me. He receives me, He doesn't reject me. He embraces me—every part of me. When we are saved, He doesn't see the dirt, He sees the blood. He sees us whole. Yes, He convicts, but He corrects us in order to direct us. The enemy condemns. A carnal mind is enmity against God. To be carnally-minded is the opposite of being spiritually-minded. The carnal mind can't receive what God says. The carnal mind is negative, always looking at things with a negative outlook. What does God say about

His children? He loves us and gave His Son for us and wants to be with us.

Embracing God is just like breathing. It's easy. The key is to allow Him to embrace us and trust Him. He isn't hung up on our flaws and sins, but the enemy will keep us bound there. In God, there is liberty and He never lets us go. Embrace His love, forgiveness, kindness, gentleness, mercy, grace, goodness and favor. That is all He has for us—not death, bad, or evil, but everything good. He is a good, good Father!

Now I have done all this talking about embrace. But embrace is just the first step in the process. Yes, it is a process and it could take a while, honestly it has taken me years. And so now after all of that embracing, you have to release. You have to release the pain, release the past, release your identity, and release your destiny.

Close your eyes, take a deep breath and blow it out. **Release it.**

It makes sense to say release the pain and release the past but to release your identity and your destiny, sounds kind of crazy. You need to release it into the hands of the Father. Release your identity because He is the one Who created you, crafted and molded you intricately in your mother's womb (Psalm 139:15). He knows you better than you know yourself. He knows your uniqueness, the very things that makes you, you. He made you for Himself. He created you for His glory. We are to be His reflection. There is no one else like you. God doesn't make duplicates, He makes originals. Nobody can be you better than you, so work to remove those things that have blocked your liberty.

Release your destiny. That means totally trusting God with your dreams, plans and life. He knows the plans He has for you. Sometimes the plans that we have for ourselves do not coincide with His plan. You may wonder why things are not going the way you hoped, it could be that you haven't released your destiny into His hands. Our focus should be on Him. If not careful, our ambitions can become more important than God and take precedence over Him which is a form of idolatry. Anything we put before God is an idol. Nothing is wrong with ambition, but is it driving us toward God and His purpose, plan and destiny for our lives or is it driving us away from Him?

> Trust in the Lord, and do good; Dwell in the land, and feed on His faithfulness. Delight yourself also in the Lord, And He shall give you the desires of your heart. Commit your way to the Lord, Trust also in Him, And He shall bring it to pass. He shall bring forth your righteousness as the light, And your justice as the noonday. Rest in the Lord, and wait patiently for Him; Do not fret because of him who prospers in his way, Because of the man who brings wicked schemes to pass. (Psalms 37:3—5 NKJV)

STEP UP AND OVER

For the past few days, I have felt discouraged and ready to throw in the towel to a lot of things. The more I was fighting and pressing, the further away some dreams and desires seemed to be. It made me begin to question my purpose for pressing on. That sounds crazy. I was thinking, why am I fighting and pressing, just enjoy the ordinary day-to-day because it will be easier that way. I get tired of fighting sometimes. Yeah, I said it. Sometimes I just want to live a normal life. Why can't I just be content or satisfied with how my life is currently going? Why from time to time does this discontentment come upon me and then things begin to be obscure? Obscurity is the quality of being difficult to understand, a thing that is unclear or difficult to understand.[3] Why aren't things happening for me? Lord what do I need to do? I am desiring you and trying to live a holy life, wholeheartedly unto You. I am trying to be a good wife, daughter, friend, sister, coworker and citizen. Lord, why aren't things happening for me? Why does it seem like it's never going to happen for me? Where are you Lord? Fill me up, Lord. I feel empty inside, Lord. Your will Lord, not mine.

On the date I was writing, it was a Sunday. I was determined to praise my way through and get a breakthrough. It was hard, I told God before church that I felt empty and I asked Him to please fill me up. "I want more of you, O God. Help me. Speak." Nothing seems to be moving forward. Things are just blah. I have felt this way before and in times past would probably stay a little longer than I should. But something in me, said "step up and over and keep pressing on." Now, I have heard step up and move forward, but the step over part was a little different. I saw myself, lift my leg to step up and over the murkiness and onward into purpose. It made me think about when you are walking and you see a puddle of mud and instead of going around it, you step over it and keep towards your destiny. We can't stay in our pity-party and expect to do great things. As world renowned tele-evangelist Joyce Meyers says, "you can either be pitiful or powerful, but you can't be both."

With so much going on in the world, if we are not careful we can find ourselves getting stuck in the murk and the mire, that place of obscurity. If we stay there long enough discouragement will come and then fear, which brings torment. The darkness can begin to seem too dark and the mud so thick that we feel that we will never be able to rise above it and overcome. It's almost like Peter, who opted to step out of the boat and walk on the water. We must not get caught up in what we are walking on or through, but focus on who we are walking toward. Peter began to drown when he took his eyes off Jesus and that is what will happen to us. When we take our eyes off Jesus, we will begin to sink.

So yes, there is a lot going on in the world and we may be wondering, "God, what am I to do? God, what are you doing?" We need to step up and over and keep pressing on. That next step is a step in faith to higher ground, to a higher place in God. Without faith, it is impossible to please God. We must have faith, we must trust God like never ever before. The assignment that He has for us must be fulfilled. He hasn't forgotten us. His time isn't our time, but He is always on time. We must continue to prepare ourselves and obey Him. God will be looking for faith when He returns, will you have it? Everything that can be shaken will be shaken. Will we be like Paul, who was able to say I finished my race (2 Timothy 4:7) or are we going to throw in the towel like the enemy wants us to do? The enemy comes to wear out the saints. But we must contend for the faith. Fight the good fight of faith. We can't grow weary in well doing. He, Who has begun a good work in you will hasten to complete it. (Philippians 1:6) We can't give up or in.

The war is on. The fight is real. Creation is eagerly waiting for the sons and daughters of God to be revealed. (Romans 8:19). Are we good soldiers? You therefore must endure hardship as a good soldier of Jesus Christ. (2 Timothy 2:3) Greater is He that is in me (you), than he that is in the world (1 John 4:4). We have work to do. We have kingdom business to do. Souls need to be reached and won for the kingdom of God. Now is not the time to be self-absorbed or to go bury your head in the sand. God has called and chosen us to be salt and light. How bright or dim is our light? It's not about us. How many times will you read that statement in this book? But we need to embrace it. Why me, you ask? Why not you is my response. Be strong. Be brave. Be courageous. God hasn't brought us this far to leave us. He has so much in store for those who believe. Be confident. If He said it, He will do it. God can't lie. God won't lie. He loves us so much. He didn't give us His Son just to save us from our sin, but so that we can live an abundant life. Abundant life isn't material things necessarily, it is living a victorious life. A life of peace. A life of joy. A life of victory. We get focused on the wrong thing and lose track of God and His awesomeness. We box Him in and don't seek His heart.

His heart is that all will be saved and come into the knowledge of Him. He just wants to be with us and for us to know Him.

He is Father. He is Abba, Papa. He sent us His Son so that the separation could be removed (wall of partition), we can come boldly before the throne of Grace. So, don't stay there, come on up a little higher. Step up and over. Go to the next level. He takes us from glory to glory (2 Corinthians 3:18). And He is expediting the process. What once seemed like it took a long time, will now be done instantly. God is waiting for us to obey and trust. Once we make up our mind and obey Him, things will shift forward. **He is waiting on our YES**. How many more excuses do we have? It's time to just trust Him and say Yes. Yes, to Your will, Lord. Yes, to Your way. Send me, I will go. The ride may be wild, but it will be glorious as He takes us higher and higher.

The enemy wants us to stay trapped and to stay in the place of obscurity so that He can set up strongholds. He wants to destroy from within. He knows that God gives and takes life, but if the devil can get our mind he knows that soon thereafter our actions will follow.

Sin is a major hindrance to your progress in the embracing process. Quit making room for the lust of the flesh. Close all doors to sin and embrace holiness. God has standards, and we can't forget His standards. When you embrace God, your desire for righteousness increases. You desire to live a holy life—a set apart life. You no longer desire to live like the world, but you desire to please the King. You desire His will and to honor Him with your life.

> Anyone who meets a testing challenge head-on and manages to stick it out is mighty fortunate. For such persons loyally in love with God, the reward is life and more life. Don't let anyone under pressure to give in to evil say, "God is trying to trip me up." God is impervious to evil, and puts

evil in no one's way. The temptation to give in to evil comes from us and only us. We have no one to blame but the leering, seducing flare-up of our own lust. Lust gets pregnant, and has a baby: sin! Sin grows up to adulthood, and becomes a real killer. So, my very dear friends, don't get thrown off course. Every desirable and beneficial gift comes out of heaven. The gifts are rivers of light cascading down from the Father of Light. There is nothing deceitful in God, nothing two-faced, nothing fickle. He brought us to life using the true Word, showing us off as the crown of all his creatures. (James 1: 12—18 MSG)

Chapter 13
It's a Process

God loves us and desires the best for us. He has the best for us. Ultimately, we have to embrace Him in order to receive what He has for us. Embrace His grace and mercy. Embrace His love. His love covers us. His love washes us and makes us whole.

In order to embrace the pain, we must repent, and allow the saving, healing, and miracle working power of God to work in our lives. Embracing the present is recognizing and examining yourself to see whether or not you are in the faith. Embracing the future is trusting God and the promises He has for you, which are so many. God is a Promise Keeper. We can trust Him with everything. He can't lie. He won't lie.

When you embrace God and the future He has for you. Your words are different. Your attitude is different and your behavior is different. All those self-defeating and doubt-filled words are no longer. The words you speak are what God says. When thoughts come to your mind that are not of hope and peace, you immediately cast them down and proclaim what God has said about you and your situation.

You walk with a confidence and boldness because you know that your Daddy sits up on the throne and He has your back. He has you covered on every side. You understand that Goodness and Mercy are following you. You know and believe that all of heaven is on your side and angels are working on your behalf to see God's promises come to fruition for you.

Your attitude is focused on God and the kingdom and you are determined not to speak out anything that is not according to the Word. You are determined to walk in holiness. You are determined to love the Lord with all that is within you.

With embracing the pain and releasing it brings freedom to embrace everything you are in Christ and everything He has for you. The more you embrace God, the more that pain, frustration, and disappointment dissipates because of the love of God. It becomes suffocated by the love and power of God.

God is greater than your pain.

God is greater than your current situation and circumstance. God is greater than anything you ask or think concerning your future.

God is greater. Why? Because He is the Great I Am.

Embrace Him and watch everything else fall into place. God will and can blow your mind. He is ready and waiting to do just that. We are His sons and daughters. Take your rightful place. Walk in power, victory, love, joy and peace. It's a process, not an easy one, but it will be worth every tear and scream. Greater, greater, greater.

Embrace by repenting of your sins and forgive those who hurt you or mislead you. Repent of those areas that haven't pleased God. Get in a Bible-believing church. Read the Word. Build yourself up on your most Holy Faith by praying in the Holy Ghost (Jude 20). Invite the Holy Spirit to have His way in you and trust God. Examine yourself and allow God to finish the work He has started in you. Trust God. He can't fail. He won't fail. **He is your #1 Fan!!!!!**

> Lord God, thank you. Thank You for being who You are. Thank You for being God and God alone. Thank

You for the past. I have been hurt, denied, rejected, taken advantage of, and so much more. But God, thank You. God, I doubted You and I doubted myself. Forgive me. Daddy, I forgive those who caused me pain. Father, I repent of all those I have caused pain. Father I repent for causing You pain. I want more of You. I want to be who You called and destined for me to be. Take out everything in me that is not like You. Show me those areas that I have yet to yield to You. God, I abandon myself to You. I trust You. I need You. Help me. Draw me.

Fill me. Fill every empty place. Purify me, wash me, cleanse me and make me whole. Create in me a clean heart and renew in me a right spirit (Psalm 51:10). Purge me with hyssop, oh God. I make you my dwelling place. Help me God to renew my mind. I hunger and thirst for your righteousness. As the deer pants for the water, so does my soul thirst for You.

Thank You. Thank You for Your power. Thank You for Your Son, Jesus Who gave His life for me. He went to the cross for my sins, took my death, and rose again with all power in His hands.

Satan, I will no longer give you power in my life. I cast down every thought and image that may exalt itself against the knowledge God.

God, I trust You. I believe You. I depend on You. I long for more You. Put Your desires in me. Make me more like You. I release all the hurt and pain and embrace You, and what You have for me.

Victory is mine!
Love is mine!
Peace in mine!
Freedom is mine!

I thank you God that it is so. In the mighty name
of Jesus!
I seal it with a praise. Hallelujah! Thank you, Jesus!

My sister and my brother, receive it. Receive what the Lord
has for you. You no longer have to walk in mediocrity. You are
more than a conqueror. God loves you. We need each other in
these last days. So stand up and take your place. Don't allow the
past or present circumstances to stop you, but use it as a stepping
stool to get what God has for you.

Exhortation 5
The Embrace of God

I thought I was finished, but I can't end this book without talking just a little bit more about the embrace of God. David said if I had a thousand tongues I couldn't thank and praise Him enough. When I think about the love of God, and His embrace I can't thank and praise Him enough. God's embrace suffocates all hurt, pain, disappointment, confusion, anger, and frustration. Everything. When I say everything, I mean **EVERYTHING.**

Rejection is at the root of all of this, and to get healed from rejection, it must be cut from the root. Rejection is cut at the root by God's embrace. **Rejection can only be erased by the love of God.** The more you allow God's love to embrace you and consume you, the more rejection is rejected. You will begin to reject the lies of the enemy and embrace what God says about you. You will reject fear and embrace bravery and confidence in God and yourself. You will reject loneliness and embrace the intimacy of God. You will reject low self-esteem and self-worth and will embrace that you are wonderfully and fearfully made. You will reject confusion and embrace God's peace and direction. You will reject feeling useless and embrace God's purpose. You will reject weakness and embrace God's strength. You will reject pain and embrace God's healing power. You will reject defeat and embrace victory. Whatever it is, you fill in the blank, and instead embrace what God says. You will no longer believe any lie the devil throws your way and you will embrace the Truth. You will reject shame and embrace the cleansing, saving power of the blood of Jesus Christ. You will reject the devil and will embrace the cross.

When you reject all the enemy says and embrace God, your praise will be for real. You will worship Him in spirit and in truth. You will honor and adore Him. You will magnify the Lord above all your circumstances. You will exalt Him. You will realize how big and great your God is versus your problems. You will no longer settle for mediocrity. You will be holy. You will seek the Lord with your whole heart. You will love God. You will love you and you will love others.

God is great and greatly to be praise. **Embrace His embrace.** Embrace your identity in Christ Jesus. The embrace of God changes you and rearranges your life. You will confidently say it was all worth it. All of it (the pain, hurt, disappointment, discomfort). You will thank Him for the pain. You will thank Him for your past. You will thank Him for your present. You will praise Him in advance for your future! You will no longer be confused about your identity. You will know who you are because of Whose you are. And you will know how loved you are by the Almighty God. I call Him, Papa, Daddy God. *You can too!*

Bibliography

1   https://en.oxforddictionaries.com/definition/embrace. (2018).
2   https://en.oxforddictionaries.com/definition/doubt. (2018).
3   https://en.oxforddictionaries.com/definition/obscurity. (2018).

About the Author

Olympia Pringle's life purpose and passion is to help others maximize their potential and live their best life. More specifically, Olympia empowers women to live life to the fullest and enjoy their journey. Her purpose is almost paradoxical because she has had a difficult journey realizing her own potential. Her own personal life struggles are why she is so zealous bout coaching people in overcoming past hurts and present chaos, and equipping them to walk in victory.

Olympia is an ordained minister, psalmist, and educator. She earned a Master's degree in Guidance and Counseling and a Master's in Human Development and Leadership from Murray State University. She has been working in higher education for over ten years in various positions within student success and academic advising. During her time in college she started a Women's Bible study (Women of Worship). She has served as praise and worship leader, mentored a number of beautiful young women, and continues to minister at churches and Christian events.

She has been married to her wonderful husband Willie for a little over 2 years. She was single for over ten years before she met and married the one God kept for her. She understands the joy and heartache of being a single Christian woman. She knows without a doubt that it is the love and power of God that keeps us and that God's love is the greatest love we could ever know. She hopes and prays that her writing will help others pull back the layers of hurt, pain and defeat. She desires everyone to know and believe that we really can do *all* things through Christ Jesus.